# HERSTORY

## 50 WOMEN AND GIRLS WHO SHOOK THE WORLD

nosy crow

For our mothers and grandmothers, our sisters
and our daughters . . . and for Holly.

K. H. and S. W.

First published 2018 by Nosy Crow Ltd
The Crow's Nest, 14 Baden Place, Crosby Row
London, SE1 1YW
www.nosycrow.com

ISBN 978 1 78800 138 0

Nosy Crow and associated logos are trademarks
and/or registered trademarks of Nosy Crow Ltd.

Text © Katherine Halligan 2018
Illustrations © Sarah Walsh 2018
For photo credits see page III.
All rights reserved.

A CIP catalogue record for this book is available from the British Library.

Printed in Turkey.
Papers used by Nosy Crow are made from wood
grown in sustainable forests.

1 3 5 7 9 8 6 4 2

# CONTENTS

Introduction — Pages 4-5

## BELIEVE & LEAD

Elizabeth I — Pages 6-7
Joan of Arc — Pages 8-9
Indira Gandhi — Pages 10-11
Theresa Kachindamoto — Pages 12-13
Empress Wu Zetian — Pages 14-15
Harriet Tubman — Pages 16-17
Boudicca — Pages 18-19
Hatshepsut — Pages 20-21
Isabella I — Pages 22-23
Sacajawea — Pages 24-25

## IMAGINE & CREATE

Frida Kahlo — Pages 26-27
Beatrix Potter — Pages 28-29
Coco Chanel — Pages 30-31
Billie Holiday — Pages 32-33
Anna Pavlova — Pages 34-35
Mirabai — Pages 36-37
Maya Angelou — Pages 38-39
Georgia O'Keeffe — Pages 40-41
Emily Brontë — Pages 42-43
Sarah Bernhardt — Pages 44-45

## HELP & HEAL

Florence Nightingale — Pages 46-47
Helen Keller — Pages 48-49
Annie Sullivan — Pages 50-51
Mary Seacole — Pages 52-53
Shirin Ebadi — Pages 54-55
Maria Montessori — Pages 56-57

Mother Teresa — Pages 58-59
Wangari Maathai — Pages 60-61
Elizabeth Blackwell — Pages 62-63
Eva Perón — Pages 64-65

## THINK & SOLVE

Marie Curie — Pages 66-67
Rachel Carson — Pages 68-69
Ada Lovelace — Pages 70-71
Hypatia — Pages 72-73
Rosalind Franklin — Pages 74-75
Mary Anning — Pages 76-77
Katherine Johnson — Pages 78-79
Dorothy Hodgkin — Pages 80-81
Dian Fossey — Pages 82-83
Valentina Tereshkova — Pages 84-85

## HOPE & OVERCOME

Malala Yousafzai — Pages 86-87
Rigoberta Menchú — Pages 88-89
Amelia Earhart — Pages 90-91
Hannah Szenes — Pages 92-93
Rosa Parks — Pages 94-95
Noor Inayat Khan — Pages 96-97
Emmeline Pankhurst — Pages 98-99
Cathy Freeman — Pages 100-101
Sophie Scholl — Pages 102-103
Anne Frank — Pages 104-105

When They Lived — Pages 106-107
Glossary — Pages 108-109
Index — Pages 110-111
Chapter Explanations — Page 112

# INTRODUCTION

> " *Every great dream begins with a dreamer. Always remember, you have within you the strength, the patience, and the passion to reach for the stars to change the world.* "
>
> Harriet Tubman

There are almost four billion women and girls in the world today. Every day, millions of them carry out acts of bravery, creativity, kindness, cleverness and hope. Most of those women and girls — and their amazing actions and achievements — remain unknown to the rest of us . . . but occasionally their acts shake the world.

History is often just 'his story': tales of kings and conquerors, of men who fought wars and built nations. But throughout human history, countless women and girls have fought in great and small ways to make their mark on the world and change the future. Many of their stories have been lost, forgotten or hidden. In this book we celebrate the lives of 50 incredible women and girls who refused to obey the rules society set for them, and whose lives, work and words can inspire us all to make the world a better place. Now it is time to talk about a past and a present that are not *his*tory, but *her*story.

This is the story of brave leaders, who believed in doing what was right for their country and their people. Some of them faced imprisonment and even death for following their beliefs. Some of them made difficult choices that made sense to them during their time, but that we might find hard to understand now. All of them proved that women were just as capable as men in positions of power, making stronger, better leaders than many of the men who came before and after them.

This is the story of talented artists, writers and performers, who changed the world with their art and with their lives. Some of them had help along the way, and some had to fight to express their ideas. All of them created beautiful works of art — in spite of, and sometimes because of, the difficulties and rejections they faced.

This is the story of gifted healers and committed teachers, who dedicated their lives to helping others. Some of them came from a place of privilege and wanted to share their good fortune with others, and some overcame unimaginable hardships themselves. All of them worked tirelessly to care for those in need, risking their health, their wealth and even their own lives to improve the lives of others.

This is the story of gifted scientists and mathematicians, who were driven by curiosity to solve the mysteries of the world around them. Some of them faced prejudice and danger. Some made great personal sacrifices, but thought that these were worthwhile in order to make discoveries that could change millions of lives. All of them had to challenge the belief that the world of science, facts and figures was a world for men, and men only.

This is the story of women and girls who followed their dreams, whatever the cost. All of them overcame challenges, faced danger and made sacrifices, and some of them even lost their lives — but they never gave up hoping to make the world a better place.

This is the story of 50 women and girls who did extraordinary things. Some of them won prizes, while others were never appreciated during their lifetimes. Some of them died tragically young, while others lived long lives. They became leaders, artists, revolutionaries, thinkers and idealists, because they knew that to turn their hopes and dreams into reality they had to shake the world . . . and so they did.

What is your dream? Take inspiration from these
50 amazing women and girls and shake things up!

# ELIZABETH I

One of England's greatest rulers
and the founder of an empire

Elizabeth's
portrait on a coin

Elizabeth as a young woman

## A TROUBLED PRINCESS

Elizabeth was born in 1533 into a time of political and royal drama. She was the daughter of King Henry VIII of England and his second wife, Anne Boleyn. Henry believed that only a man could rule a nation and dramatically divorced his first wife, Catherine of Aragon, with whom he had a daughter but no sons, so he could marry Anne. When Anne's baby turned out to be a girl too, Henry was disappointed.

Henry quickly found another new bride, Jane Seymour, and had Anne Boleyn executed as a traitor. But Jane soon died giving birth to Elizabeth's younger brother, Edward. Elizabeth's father next married Anne of Cleves, whom he divorced almost immediately. He then married his fifth wife, Catherine Howard, Anne Boleyn's cousin. She too was executed by the impatient king, who finally married Katherine Parr before he died himself. Elizabeth was 13, and Edward just nine when he took the throne.

Young Elizabeth watched all of this from afar and clearly learnt her lesson: marriage was a dangerous thing for a woman. She was determined not to be ruled by any man, in case she ended up like her mother and stepmothers — set aside, forgotten or even killed. Luckily, her last stepmother, Katherine Parr, was a kind woman who ensured that the young princess was educated just as well as if she had been a prince.

**" I would rather be a beggar and single than a queen and married. "**

Known as the 'Virgin Queen'

**" You will nevertheless find me a rock that bends to no wind. "**

When Edward, aged only 15, became ill and died, Elizabeth's older sister, Mary, took the throne. Mary was a devout Catholic and Elizabeth was a Protestant, and because of this Mary declared Elizabeth to be her enemy, locking her up in the Tower of London.

## RULING ALONE

When Mary died, Elizabeth inherited the throne at the age of 25. Being Queen of England was a tough job: England was poor, and fighting between Catholics and Protestants meant it was deeply divided. Elizabeth quickly made England a Protestant nation once more, but unlike her sister before her, she allowed her subjects to practise their own faiths quietly.

Hatfield House in England, where Elizabeth learned she was to be Queen of England

With a new queen on the throne, suitors appeared from all over Europe. But only one man came close to capturing Elizabeth's heart: Robert Dudley, Earl of Leicester. However, she was determined not to marry, even for love. Although Parliament refused to give her the money she needed to rule unless she married, she resisted: she would rule England alone.

> **"I know I have the body of a weak and feeble woman, but I have the heart and stomach of a king, and of a king of England too."**

Under Elizabeth, English culture flourished and William Shakespeare's plays started a Golden Age of literature. She also looked beyond English borders, sending Francis Drake to sail around the globe. In America, her knight Sir Walter Raleigh started a colony named Virginia, after the unmarried 'Virgin Queen'. An empire had begun, and soon money and goods from the new colonies came pouring into the royal treasury.

Elizabeth's position was not always safe. There were many plots to overthrow her, including one involving her cousin, Mary Queen of Scots. After Elizabeth had Mary executed for treason, Mary's supporter, Philip II of Spain, sent a huge fleet of ships to invade England, known as the Spanish Armada. But Elizabeth's own fleet — helped by strong winds — pushed them back, and England was safe again.

Elizabeth's unique signature. The 'R' stands for Regina, which is the Latin for queen.

## SHAKING THE WORLD

Elizabeth ruled for 45 years. Many people believe that she was the greatest monarch ever to rule England. Where there had been violence and poverty, she created peace and prosperity. She sponsored the arts and the exploration of the New World, starting an empire that would last for hundreds of years. And she did all of this on her own, resisting a marriage that might have made it harder for her to rule in her own right.

# JOAN OF ARC

Army leader, martyr and saint

## A DANGEROUS CHILDHOOD

Joan of Arc (or Jeanne d'Arc in her native French) was born around the year 1412 in Domrémy in France. Her parents were poor peasant farmers. Her mother was very religious, and passed on to Joan an unshakable faith in God and the saints of the Catholic church. Joan's father taught Joan to take care of the animals on her family's farm, while her mother taught her to sew, and Joan became an excellent seamstress.

But Joan's childhood was short. The area around her home was a dangerous place, as French and English armies fought over who would rule France in what became known as the Hundred Years' War.

> **"I am not afraid ... I was born to do this."**

**Vive la France**

**The Maid of Orléans**

## VISIONS AND VICTORY

When Joan was 13, she began having mystical visions. She believed that the saints were talking to her. Her visions made her believe that she would help the French prince, Charles, known as the Dauphin, claim back his throne from the English invaders. When Joan first approached a local military commander to ask to meet with the Dauphin, she was laughed at and turned away. But the following year, with the support of two of the commander's soldiers, she tried again.

At this meeting, Joan told the commander that her visions had revealed the Dauphin's army was in trouble, near the besieged town of Orléans. Days later, a messenger arrived to confirm the news. The commander was so impressed that he gave Joan a horse and soldiers to travel with her to meet the Dauphin. She cut her hair short and dressed in men's clothes for the journey.

But how could a poor peasant girl, who couldn't even read or write, lead the French army against the English enemy? At first the Dauphin was suspicious, but after his priests tested Joan they found that she was faithful and humble and honest, so Charles decided to give her a chance.

Dressed in a suit of armour and riding a huge white horse, Joan led the Dauphin's army to Orléans where the French, who had been losing for so long, finally managed to beat the English. Two of Joan's brothers, Jean and Pierre, fought with their sister, who became known as the Maid of Orléans. Thanks to Joan's bravery, the Dauphin was soon crowned King Charles VII. She was the hero of all of France.

Statue of Joan in Winchester Cathedral, England

> **" I would rather die than do something which I know to be a sin, or to be against God's will. "**

But around a year later, Joan was captured and handed over to the English. She was put on trial and accused of many crimes including dressing like a man and being a witch. Although Charles was angry about Joan's capture, he was unable to save her. Joan was found guilty and after a year in prison, was burned at the stake. A crowd of 10,000 people came to watch as their hero was put to death. She was 19 years old.

## SHAKING THE WORLD

Twenty-two years after Joan's death, the war ended and Charles VII kept his crown. He declared that Joan was innocent and called her a martyr. Nearly 500 years later, Joan was made a saint by the Catholic church and is now the patron saint of France. Her feast day is 30th May, the day she died. Although some people have tried to make Joan into a patriotic symbol of France and France alone, her bravery and belief do not belong to just one group of people: she is an example to everyone, from all backgrounds and beliefs, of how the courage of one person can change the world.

ST JOAN

> **" If I am not, may God put me there; and if I am, may God so keep me. "**

# INDIRA GANDHI

The first ever woman to be elected to lead a country

## HER FATHER'S DAUGHTER

Born in 1917, Indira was the only child of the man who became the first Indian prime minister, Jawaharlal Nehru. While she was growing up, her father was helping to lead the fight for independence from the British, who had controlled India for nearly 200 years. Her mother Kamala gave speeches when her husband was in prison, and was also arrested by the British because of how popular she was becoming with women's groups around India.

Indira as a young girl

With her father often away and her mother often ill, Indira was a lonely child. Inspired by Joan of Arc and by Mahatma Gandhi, the man who had started the independence movement in India, she tried to help by involving school children in the campaign to free India from the British with posters and other demonstrations.

Indira was extremely intelligent and after being taught at home, she went to many different schools in India, Switzerland and England. Sadly, her mother died of tuberculosis when Indira was 19 years old. Indira, who was living in England, was comforted by a friend called Feroze Gandhi (who was not related to Mahatma Gandhi). They were married a few years later in India.

Indira Priyadarshini Nehru Gandhi

" Actions today mould our tomorrows. "

## WINNING AND LOSING

India was going through huge changes and, finally in 1947, it became independent from Britain. Indira's father was chosen as the country's first prime minister. As his wife had died, Indira helped her father, acting as his 'first lady', assistant and hostess — and learning a lot about politics as she did so.

After he died in 1964, the next prime minister, Lal Bahadur Shastri, appointed Indira as minister of information and broadcasting. In her new job, Indira did something brave: she allowed people of all backgrounds and beliefs to speak on the television and radio, even those who didn't agree with the government. For the first time in India, people were allowed to speak freely.

Two years later, Shastri died, and Indira became prime minister until the next election, when she became the first woman in the world to be elected as leader of a country by its people. She was elected four times in total, but not everyone was happy with her leadership. India was a divided country with many different groups fighting with one another. She was forced to give up power and even went to prison before she was re-elected for the fourth time. That same year, the younger of her two sons was killed in a plane crash. She made some very tough decisions to try to bring unity and peace to India, some of which resulted in many deaths. Because of this, some people believed that she was too ruthless, but many others admired her strength and determination.

**"You cannot shake hands with a clenched fist."**

Then, in 1984, two of her own bodyguards shot and killed her, shocking the world. She had known there was danger all around her, and the night before she died she had said, "I don't mind if my life goes in the service of the nation. If I die today, every drop of my blood will invigorate the nation."

**"If you're feeling helpless, help someone."**

## SHAKING THE WORLD

Indira made India a more modern and powerful country, leading it to victory in a war against Pakistan and helping to create the new country of Bangladesh. She helped India launch its first satellite into space, and worked hard to help the millions of poor people in her country. And she started a Green Revolution that aimed to create more jobs and enough food for all of the people of India.

She led her country for many years during difficult times, and made life better for many of India's people. She became a symbol of strength for women all over the world, as a brave and inspiring leader.

Indira and her father, Jawaharlal Nehru

**"I would say our greatest achievement is to have survived as a free and democratic nation."**

# THERESA KACHINDAMOTO

Theresa leading the campaign to end violence against women and girls

### RELUCTANT LEADER

Theresa Kachindamoto was the youngest of 12 children, born in 1958 into a family of chiefs in the Dedza District near Lake Malawi. Because she was the youngest sibling, a busy working mother of five, and a daughter in a world where normally only men become chiefs, Theresa never imagined she would become a senior tribal leader.

> **" If you educate your girls, you will have everything in the future. "**

Theresa Kachindamoto

But when the chiefs called her home, supposedly because she was 'good with people', she left her job at a college — one she had held for 27 years — and headed home to put on the red robes, beads and leopard skin headdress of a senior chief. Theresa became the Inkosi of the Chidyaonga line of the Maseko or Gomani dynasty — an impressive title for a modest, mild-mannered former secretary.

## CHANGING GIRLS' LIVES

As she started visiting the homes of the people who were now suddenly under her command, Theresa decided she would use her authority over 900,000 people to change things for the better. Malawi is one of the poorest countries in the world. Poverty means that it's easier for parents to marry their daughters off than to have another mouth to feed.

Theresa was shocked when she saw that girls as young as 12 were having babies. In fact, Malawi had one of the highest child marriage rates in the world; one out of two girls were married before 18. In Malawi, there are many serious problems, including violence against girls and women, early pregnancies, young mothers dying of complications in childbirth because their bodies are too small, and low numbers of girls getting into and staying in education.

Combined with a culture of silence, where abuse by fathers and husbands is accepted as normal, this means a dark future for girls in Malawi.

Or it did, until Theresa spoke out. Determined to change things for Malawian girls, she first banned traditional practices that put young girls at risk of abuse. When she discovered that people were unwilling to change old habits, she used the law to tell 50 sub-chiefs they had to sign an agreement to break up existing child marriages and ban any future ones, "whether you like it or not". Four of them resisted, so she suspended them until they agreed. Over the last few years, she has dissolved over 850 child marriages in the Dedza District, freeing those children to return to education.

## SHAKING THE WORLD

Theresa wants children, especially girls, to go to school. She has created a network of parents to watch the situation closely and ensure that children stay in school. Things are slowly changing, but it has not been easy: Theresa has even received death threats from those who do not want to abandon the old ways. She has shrugged them off in her calm, gentle manner and just quotes the law back at them. When there is no public money available to send the children to school, Theresa pays for them to go out of her own pocket.

> **"If they are educated, they can be and have whatever they want."**

Children learning English at a school in Malawi

Theresa brings female Malawian MPs to the villages to inspire young girls and to show them what is possible if they stay in school. As a result, students have become very interested in learning English, which is Malawi's official language. She also takes girls on trips to the city, so that they can see there is a world beyond the traditional farming ways of life.

She is now working to raise the legal age for marriage from 18 to 21, to improve girls' opportunities for education even further. This, she believes, is the only way to break the cycle of poverty in Malawi. Theresa continues to dedicate her life to improving the future not just of the girls and young women in her tribe, but to making a better future for the whole country.

> **"Educate a girl and you educate the whole area. You educate the world."**

# EMPRESS WU ZETIAN

## LUCKY START

Wu Zetian was born in AD 624 in the Shanxi province of China. The Wu family was wealthy and her father Wu Shihuo was a chancellor for the Tang Dynasty. Unusually for the time, he encouraged his clever daughter to read, write, play music and speak in public — skills normally taught only to boys. Her father raised her to believe that women could do anything that men could do.

Both bright and beautiful, 14-year-old Zetian was noticed by Emperor Taizong, who invited her to his court and gave her the important responsibility of the royal laundry. One day, she bravely spoke to the emperor, who was impressed by her intelligence, and he decided to make her his secretary instead. Even though she was young, she helped with important business of the empire, and Zetian was good at her new job.

> **❝** The ideal ruler is one who rules like a mother rules over her children. **❞**

Also known as Wu Zhao and Wu Hou

## EMPRESS OF HEAVEN

The emperor's oldest son noticed beautiful Zetian, too — and fell in love with her. After Taizong died, the prince became Emperor Gaozong. Even though he was already married, he loved Zetian and they had two sons together. Gaozong's first wife, Lady Wang, was furious. After Zetian had a daughter, the poor baby was found dead in her cot. Wu Zetian believed Lady Wang had killed her. Lady Wang was accused of witchcraft, divorced by the emperor, banished, then killed.

Wu Zetian became the first wife of the emperor and China's new empress. Soon after, there was a huge earthquake, which many people believed to be a bad omen proving that a woman should not rule. Her husband had bad eyesight and struggled to read, so Zetian took on more and more of the work of leading China.

When Gaozong started calling himself 'Emperor of Heaven', Zetian called herself 'Empress of Heaven': she knew that she was equal to any man.

When Gaozong died, the empress made first her elder and then her younger son emperor, ruling from behind the scenes, but when they did not obey her, she forced them to give up the throne, proclaiming herself Emperor of China. Ruling China with absolute power, she renamed the dynasty 'Tianzhou', or 'granted by heaven', claiming that she was a divine ruler. She created new characters for the Chinese alphabet: even the way people wrote would change under her reign.

China was the first country to produce silk from silkworms, which it traded with the West along the Silk Road

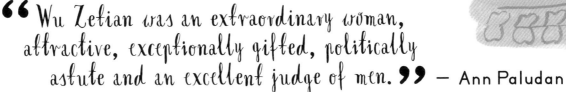

> **Wu Zetian was an extraordinary woman, attractive, exceptionally gifted, politically astute and an excellent judge of men.** — Ann Paludan

And many things did change, often for the better. China had long been a land where many leaders were not trustworthy, lying and cheating to keep their power. Wu Zetian decided to end all of this. She started a system of spies so that she always knew what was happening. She fired many government officials, saving money and making the kingdom run more smoothly. She created a special box where people could send suggestions directly to the emperor, and she used many of her people's ideas, making herself very popular. She changed the education system, hiring the best possible teachers and introducing exams so that all workers in the government or military had to prove their intelligence. She reopened the Silk Road to start trade with the West, bringing money to China. She improved farming — and the lives of her people — by lowering taxes and encouraging people to grow bigger crops. And she shared out the land so that everyone had a small, equal piece to farm.

## SHAKING THE WORLD

Wu Zetian ruled for many years, and she was known by many names, but one thing is clear: she made China a fairer and more peaceful place. Although many historians have shown her as a ruthless, cruel politician, she proved that women were equal to men, and that they could rule just as well — or indeed better.

Her tomb marker is blank, possibly because people were uncomfortable honouring a woman who held such power. Other stories say she believed her successes were so impressive words could not describe them; while some believe she wanted her actions to be judged by later generations. Although her enemies accused her of many crimes, people now recognise the many positive changes she made to her country and to the lives of ordinary people.

A portrait of Wu Zetian as an older woman

# HARRIET TUBMAN

Anti-slavery freedom fighter

## SLAVE CHILD

Araminta Ross was born as a slave in Maryland, USA, around the year 1820. Her exact birthday is unknown, because slaves were not valued as people and so their birthdays were rarely written down. She later changed her name to Harriet, which was her mother's name. When she was around five, she was sent to work as a house slave, but at around 12, she was sent to work in the fields. Field slaves were beaten regularly. Once, while trying to protect another slave from a cruel beating, Harriet was hit on the head by a heavy weight. She never fully recovered from the injury, which sometimes made her suddenly fall deeply asleep.

A portrait of Harriet as an older woman

## ROAD TO FREEDOM

In 1849, Harriet fled on foot. Helped by a friendly white woman, Harriet followed the North Star through the woods at night, towards the northern states where slavery was illegal and African Americans were free. But, safe in the North, Harriet worried about those she'd left behind — her husband, her parents, her brothers and sisters — and so, incredibly, she went back.

First she led her sister and her sister's children to freedom, and then returned to rescue her brother and two others. On one of her most dangerous journeys, she led her elderly parents north. Harriet returned to the South at least 19 times during the 1850s, risking her life to free other slaves, and becoming the most famous conductor on the Underground Railroad. The Underground Railroad was a secret network of safe houses and kind people throughout the South and into the North.

> **There was one of two things I had a right to, liberty or death; if I could not have one, I would have the other.**

Harriet helped the Railroad to grow, coming up with clever tricks for her brave rescues. She made her journeys on Saturday nights, because notices about escaped slaves weren't printed in newspapers until Monday; she used secret codes in letters and hooted like an owl to signal when it was safe to move; she carried medicine to make babies sleep so they wouldn't cry. The journeys were long and difficult — but always safe.

She led many dozens of slaves to freedom, and was proud of the fact that she "never lost a single passenger". Frightened slaves felt brave with Harriet leading the way, and Harriet felt brave because she believed that God was protecting her.

During the American Civil War, Harriet continued her work in the fight for freedom, as a nurse on the battlefields and as a scout and a spy for the North's Union Army. Harriet herself led a group of black soldiers, passing on knowledge to the Union Army and guiding a famous expedition that freed over 700 slaves.

A portrait of Harriet by William H Johnson

The Union Army only paid Harriet $200 (around £140) for her work. Yet slave owners offered rewards for her capture up to $40,000 — nearly £1,000,000 in today's money. The average price of a slave in 1850 was around £300, so the slave holders placed a value on Harriet that was many times what they had paid for the people she saved.

**" My people must go free. "**

It is impossible to put a real value on someone's life: life and freedom are priceless. But this shows Harriet's incredible power as a freedom fighter: she made slave owners realise that slaves could rebel against their captivity, and she gave slaves hope that they might one day escape.

Harriet Tubman

**" Every great dream begins with a dreamer. "**

## SHAKING THE WORLD

After the war, when slavery was finally ended throughout the whole of the United States and nearly four million slaves were set free, Harriet moved to New York State where she cared for her parents and other elderly freed slaves in her home, earning money to care for them by selling her book and giving speeches.

Known as the 'Moses' of African-American history — leading her people to freedom just as Moses did in the Bible — Harriet was many things: a civil rights pioneer, a scout, a spy, a nurse and — most importantly — a conductor on the Underground Railroad. To hundreds of slaves she gave freedom, and to those who were not yet free, she gave hope.

# BOUDICCA

## ROMAN RULE

Boudicca was born around the year AD 30 into the Iceni tribe, a Celtic people who lived in the area of England now known as East Anglia. Little is known about Boudicca's early years, but it is believed that she was the daughter of a powerful local chief. At the time she was born, the Romans had taken charge of much of Britain. Their rule was generally peaceful, but the Romans controlled most of the land that had once belonged to the native tribes. The Iceni, like the rest of the Britons, were very proud and they were not very happy to be ruled by outsiders.

## WARRIOR QUEEN

Around AD 48, Boudicca married Prasutagus, king of the Iceni people, who was a strong, independent leader and a friend of Rome. Even so, the Iceni had to pay the Romans taxes and some were even made Roman slaves. Boudicca and Prasutagus, who lived in what is now Norfolk, had two daughters. Prasutagus fairly and sensibly divided his property and money so that when he died, the two girls would inherit part and the rest would pass to Rome, in keeping with Roman law.

The Iceni area of England

However, when Prasutagus died, the Roman commanders decided to take all of his property as well as that of other Iceni leaders. Because Prasutagus had debts that Boudicca was unable to pay, the Romans beat her in public, and then attacked her daughters. Boudicca was furious and wanted revenge — and so did her people.

Tall and commanding, Boudicca was a powerful figure. She began to gather support against the Romans. The local tribes were often at war with each other, but Boudicca convinced them to unite against their common enemy, the Romans, who had treated so many tribes unfairly. Boudicca succeeded in doing what no king before her had done: she brought the Britons together.

In AD 61, Boudicca and the Britons she led set off for the Roman city of Camulodunum, which is now Colchester. A symbol of Roman power, with a great temple to the Roman emperor Claudius, Colchester did not have many soldiers to protect it and Boudicca and her followers flattened it. They then moved on to destroy Londinium, which is now London, followed by the important town of Verulamium, which is now St Albans.

Also known as Boudicea

Around 80,000 Romans and their supporters were killed by Boudicca and the Britons, who dealt harshly with anyone left behind. The Romans were ashamed, and even more upset that the raids were led by a woman. Boudicca seemed unstoppable.

After conquering Colchester, London and St Albans, Boudicca and her army moved north. They ambushed a large group of Roman soldiers on the way, ready to beat their enemy once more. They met the troops of the Roman governor Suetonius in open battle. Although there were far more Britons, they were soon trapped, surrounded by Romans who had had better training, discipline and weapons. The Romans stopped the first wave of Britons with javelins, and the second wave with short swords and shields.

It was a terrible defeat for Boudicca's followers: only 400 Romans were killed in the Battle of Watling Street, but over 200,000 Britons died. Boudicca is believed to have died either from her wounds or from taking poison to avoid being captured. Although Boudicca's rebellion had nearly forced the Romans out of England, in the end the Romans won.

A statue of Boudicca in her war chariot next to the Houses of Parliament in London, England

> **“I am not fighting for my kingdom and wealth now. I am fighting as an ordinary person for my lost freedom.”**

## SHAKING THE WORLD

Nearly 2,000 years later, Boudicca has become a legendary leader whose life and actions have inspired many poems, plays, paintings and stories. Although much of her life is surrounded by myth and mystery, we do know that she achieved an incredible thing: in a time when women were not usually leaders, she managed to do what no man had done, uniting the warring Celtic tribes and leading them successfully against three of the greatest Roman cities in England. She remains a symbol of strength, intelligence and bravery — not just for British women, but for all women.

# HATSHEPSUT
## Powerful ancient Egyptian pharaoh

## UNFAIR INHERITANCE

Hatshepsut was born over 3,500 years ago in Thebes, a great city of ancient Egypt. It was a time of huge power and wealth for the rulers, and her father Thutmose I was famous for his military strength. Hatshepsut adored him.

When Thutmose died, Hatshepsut was around 12 years old. Tradition said that the throne must go to a son, even though she was Thutmose's eldest child and the daughter of his queen, Ahmes. So the son of a less important wife inherited the throne instead. Princess Hatshepsut's name meant 'She is First Among Noble Women' — but she was forced to take second place.

> **My mouth is effective in its speech: I do not go back on my word.**

## RIGHTFUL RULER

Hatshepsut then married the new pharaoh, Thutmose II. Although today we find it strange to think of siblings marrying each other, ancient Egyptians believed this kept the royal line pure. She and Thutmose II had just one daughter, Neferu-Ra, and so, when Thutmose II died young, once again the throne went to the son of a lesser wife. But because Thutmose III was too young to rule, Hatshepsut became regent, ruling the kingdom in his place.

Then, after seven years, Hatshepsut did something that had never been done before: she named herself pharaoh. Hatshepsut knew she had to protect her throne carefully, since what she had done was so extraordinary . . . so she did something very unusual: she made sure that she was shown as a man with a beard and strong muscles in all her paintings and statues. In the many writings about her, she is described as a woman, and she is shown as a woman in earlier artwork — so she wasn't trying to make anyone think she was a man; instead, she was showing her people that she was as powerful and strong as any man.

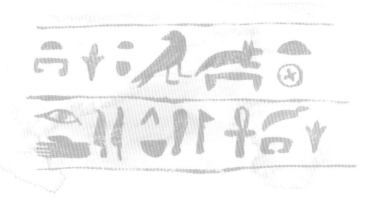

> **My command stands firm like the mountains.**

A portrait of Hatshepsut with a pharaoh's beard inside the Temple of Hatshepsut, Egypt

Hatshepsut cleverly went about proving that she was the rightful pharaoh. She strengthened her position by marrying her daughter to Thutmose III. She had artwork made that showed her father making her his co-ruler. She also claimed that she was the daughter of Amun, king of the gods, which made Hatshepsut a demi-goddess.

And she was a very good pharaoh. Constructing some of the greatest buildings in ancient Egypt, including the beautiful temple Deir al-Bahri, she built more than any pharaoh before her, creating jobs and showing her wealth and power. She started many trading expeditions, bringing back gold, incense and other riches, creating great wealth for her kingdom.

## SHAKING THE WORLD

When Hatshepsut died, her long and peaceful reign came to an end. She was buried in the Valley of the Kings, next to her father, whose sarcophagus she had moved to prove her rightful place as his heir. Many years later, Thutmose III had most of the public statues of her destroyed, perhaps because he wanted to erase from everyone's minds the possibility of another woman ever taking power.

Whatever the reason, she disappeared from history until 1829, when Jean-François Champollion — most famous for decoding the Rosetta Stone — was puzzled by the difference between hieroglyphs that talked about her as a woman and images that showed her as a man. As more of her imagery was found, Champollion and others began to discover the truth about Hatshepsut's incredible story.

In a land where very few women ruled over thousands of years, Hatshepsut proved that a woman could rule, and rule better than the men who came before her. She took power quickly and decisively, and cleverly strengthened her position, making sure that there was no question about her leadership. She ruled fairly, peacefully and well, making Egypt a stronger, better, more beautiful place . . . and becoming one of the greatest pharaohs — and indeed leaders — in history.

> **"Now my heart turns this way and that, as I think what the people will say — those who shall see my monuments in years to come, and who shall speak of what I have done."**

Her name meant 'She is First Among Noble Women'.

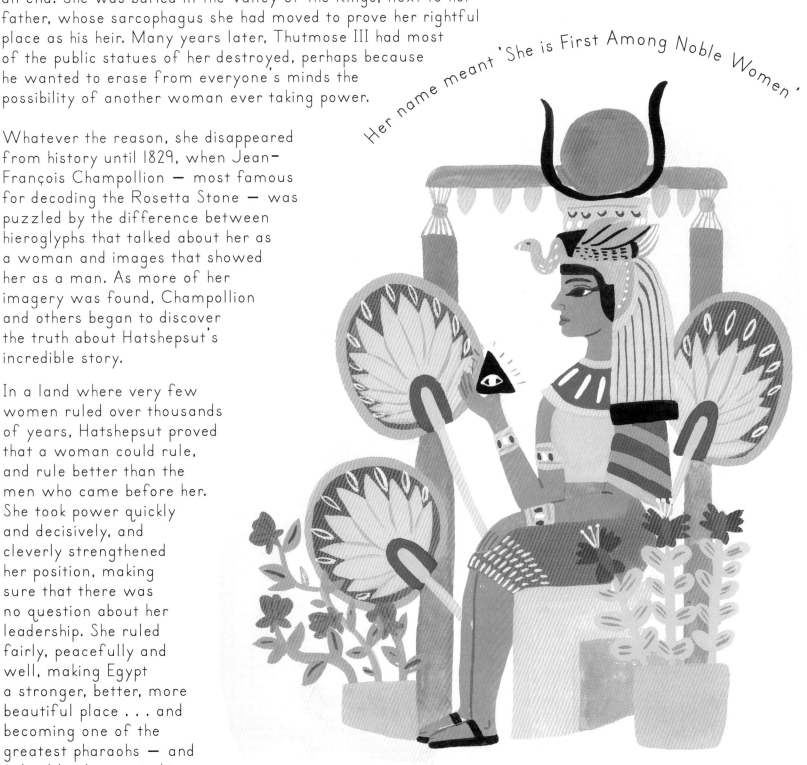

21

# ISABELLA I

**Spanish queen who united her country and started an empire**

## BORN TO RULE

Born in 1451, Isabella was the daughter of King Juan II of Castile and Isabel of Portugal. At that time, Spain was not a single country, but was divided into several different regions, and the two most powerful were Castile and Aragon. Her father died when she was three, so most of her childhood was spent quietly with her mother away from court, where the intelligent little girl was given an excellent education.

The initials of King Ferdinand and Queen Isabella (Isabel or 'Ysabella' in Spanish)

*Known as 'Isabel I de Castilla' in Spanish*

Throughout most of history, marriages were not made for love, but were arranged — especially for royalty. When her half-brother King Henry made Isabella his heiress, other European princes rushed to marry her. But Isabella bravely ignored the king's wishes and, in 1469, she married Ferdinand of Aragon, whom she liked best. When Henry died soon after, there was a war over the throne, but she and her husband triumphed, bringing Castile and Aragon together to unite almost all of Spain as one country.

> 66 *The distance is great from the firm belief to the realisation from concrete experience.* 99

## CONQUEST AND EMPIRE

Isabella and Ferdinand famously agreed to rule as equals, saying: "*Tanto monta, monta tanto*", which meant that they were opposite but equal. This was very unusual for the time, when most queens were ruled by their husbands and did not have real power.

Spain still had many problems, though, and things were not easy for the young new queen. For nearly 800 years, southern Spain had been ruled by the Muslim Moors from North Africa, a highly civilised and educated people. But Isabella and Ferdinand wanted to bring the whole country together as one, fighting a war to push the Moors out of Spain.

Isabella with Ferdinand and their royal subjects

Isabella was fascinated by military strategy and was very involved in the war. She lived at the front in a tent like her soldiers, raising her youngest daughter, Catherine, there, riding out to review the troops, and establishing military hospitals to help wounded soldiers. Finally, after 10 years of fighting, Isabella and Ferdinand pushed out the last Moors from Granada on 2 January 1492.

With Spain unified, Isabella looked outward. An Italian explorer named Christopher Columbus wanted to find a new trading route to the East Indies, so Isabella herself paid for his three ships. In fact, he found what is now known as the West Indies, claiming the land for the Spanish queen and its people as her subjects. He brought back some of the native people as slaves, but Isabella set them free.

She was not always generous and kind, though, and under her reign, the terrible Spanish Inquisition began. The Catholic church used its great power to force any Muslims or Jews who did not convert to Christianity to leave Spain. This was a huge loss to Spanish culture, and made the country a place where very strict, traditional Catholic values ruled everyone's lives for hundreds of years.

Her reign was a mixed one, because although she did things we strongly disagree with now, she also introduced many changes to help women and the poor. She pushed for better education for women, and also improved the way prisons were run, making sure that poor people had the right to be defended by a lawyer paid for by the government. Although she and Ferdinand treated Muslims and Jews terribly, in other ways she made the lives of ordinary Catholic people better.

## SHAKING THE WORLD

Even though many of her decisions were harsh and today we believe them to be wrong, Isabella was a strong ruler. She had unusual power for a woman, and used it to unite a vast area of land with many cultural differences into one great country. Her interest in the world beyond Spain started a vast empire, and she was deeply concerned about ensuring fair treatment for the native peoples of her new lands.

She also encouraged equal education for women, and appointed two female professors to the universities that flourished under her reign. She raised her four daughters to become queens of Portugal, Spain and England, passing on a legacy of strong leadership in a time when women were normally followers and not leaders.

**" I will assume the undertaking for my own crown of Castile, and am ready to pawn my jewels to defray the expenses of it. "**

# SACAJAWEA

Native American explorer and guide

## EARLY YEARS

Sacajawea was born around 1788 to the chief of the Shoshone tribe of Native Americans, in the Rocky Mountains of what is now the state of Idaho, USA. When Sacajawea was around 11 years old, their village was raided by the Hidatsa tribe, who stole most of their horses and kidnapped Sacajawea. They went north, too far for Sacajawea to attempt escape and too dangerous for her family to rescue her. At 15, she was sold to a French-Canadian trader, Toussaint Charbonneau, and became his wife.

**" Don't go around saying the world owes you a living. "**

Also known as Sacagawea

## EXPLORATION AND FREEDOM

The United States of America was a very new country at the time, and its third president, Thomas Jefferson, wanted to make it bigger. In 1803, he bought a vast piece of land from the French, known as the Louisiana Purchase, which doubled America's size. The land did not really belong to either government, but to the native peoples who lived there. Jefferson respected them, though, and wanted to explore the new territory peacefully, so he chose Meriwether Lewis and William Clark to lead a mission of scientific discovery.

**" Everything I do is for my people. "**

The Lewis and Clark expedition began in May 1804. After reaching Hidatsa lands, the explorers needed an interpreter to help them buy horses from the Shoshone. Sacajawea got the job. She spoke Shoshone with the local tribes, then translated into Hidatsa, which her husband Charbonneau translated into French, and another explorer translated into English. This was complicated, but it worked. And something else made Sacajawea an ideal guide: she had a baby. This reassured any tribes they met that the explorers came in peace, for a war party would never have a woman in it, and especially not a woman with a baby.

Meriwether Lewis and William Clark

Sacajawea and tiny Jean Baptiste led the way along mountain trails she remembered from childhood. Many of the tribes they met had never seen a white person, but Sacajawea showed them that the explorers were to be trusted. When their boat nearly capsized, Sacajawea calmly rescued important papers. Lewis and Clark were impressed by the hardworking teenager. Praised as their 'pilot', she collected plants for food and medicine, keeping the explorers well-fed and healthy.

Statue of Sacajawea and Jean Baptiste in Idaho, USA

Then she had a surprise reward: the expedition met a Shoshone tribe led by Sacajawea's brother Cameahwait! The new chief and his long-lost sister had a joyous reunion before Sacajawea bid him farewell, guiding the explorers on to the Pacific coast. When they decided where to camp for winter, she and Clark's slave, York, voted too, probably the first time a woman and an African-American man voted in the USA — and yet another sign of Lewis and Clark's respect for her.

Although she was treated as an equal by the men she had led and helped, Sacajawea received no payment for her work, while her husband was given 320 acres (1.3 square kilometres) of land and $500. It must have been hard for Sacajawea, after the equality and freedom of the expedition, to return to normal life, where Native American women were not treated well. Six years later, she had a daughter named Lisette, but Sacajawea died of a fever shortly afterwards, at the age of 25. Clark kindly adopted her children. Jean Baptiste was well educated, travelling to Europe before becoming a wilderness guide, but nothing more is known of Lisette.

> " Amazing the things you find when you bother to search for them. "

## SHAKING THE WORLD

Although Sacajawea's life was brief, it was dramatic and extraordinary. She was an important leader on a major historic expedition in American history, guiding Lewis and Clark on their famous exploration of the western United States. A teenager and a young mother, she faced danger calmly and bravely, successfully leading the men peacefully through unknown territory. She is a powerful figure in American history, a valuable guide and a bold trailblazer.

# FRIDA KAHLO

## HAPPY CHILDHOOD

Frida's German-Jewish father, Guillermo, and her Mexican mother, Matilde, were loving parents who wanted their four daughters to follow their dreams. The family all lived together in the Casa Azul, or Blue House, in Mexico City in Mexico, where Frida was born in 1907 and lived for most of her life.

When Frida was six, she got polio and had to stay in bed for nearly a year. Afterwards, she walked with a limp, but her father encouraged her to play football, swim and wrestle to help strengthen her body. These sports were unusual for girls at that time, but they helped to make Frida fit and confident.

Frida was clever, and one of the few girls at her high school. She was loved by her friends for being warm, jolly and stylish: she liked wearing traditional Mexican clothes and jewellery.

Magdalena Carmen Frida Kahlo y Calderón

## TRAGEDY AND TRIUMPH

One day, when Frida was 18, she was travelling on a bus that crashed into a tram, killing several people. A metal handrail smashed right through Frida's body and she nearly died.

Frida was in hospital for many weeks, and was changed by the accident. She still liked to joke, but she was often in pain and being stuck in bed for months while she recovered left her bored and sad. She decided to start painting, and her father helped her hang a mirror over her bed so she could paint a portrait of herself lying down.

> "Feet, what do I need you for, when I have wings to fly?"

She began painting all the time, and once she was well enough to see people again, she met and fell in love with famous Mexican artist Diego Rivera. Frida called Diego, who was very big and not very handsome, 'Sapo', which means 'toad' in Spanish. Although they loved each other deeply and were soon married, they often argued and spent a lot of time apart, living in separate houses joined by a walkway. Frida wanted a baby very much but, because of her injuries from the crash she couldn't have one. Many of her paintings are inspired by her sadness about it.

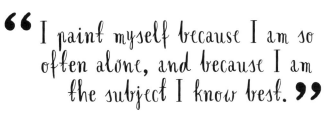

Frida painting from her bed

> **❝ I paint myself because I am so often alone, and because I am the subject I know best. ❞**

Frida loved animals, and she had many pets who brightened her life. These included a deer called Granizo, an eagle named Gertrudis Caca Blanca, (which means Gertrude White Poo!), a spider monkey called Fulang Chang, and many little dogs, her favourite of which was called Mr Xoloti. Both Fulang Chang and Mr Xoloti appear in many of her paintings.

Frida and Diego Rivera

Diego became jealous that Frida and her paintings were becoming so famous. She was invited to show her artwork in New York, USA, and Paris, France. They divorced in 1939, but then got married again the next year.

Like her husband, Frida was a Communist, believing that workers and other poor people deserved a better life. She was a close friend of the Russian revolutionary Leon Trotsky. Unlike Diego, whose art was often about politics, Frida's artwork was more personal, although she also painted about peace. Of her 143 paintings, 55 were self-portraits. She often painted herself as harsh and unattractive, with heavy eyebrows and a moustache.

As Frida grew in fame and popularity, her health grew worse and worse. She had over 30 operations in her life to help correct the problems from her awful accident, and she lived in constant pain. After a battle with pneumonia, Frida died at the age of 47.

> **❝ I am not sick, I am not broken. But I am happy to be alive as long as I can paint. ❞**

## SHAKING THE WORLD

Frida has become known and loved all over the world for her unique artwork and her paintings, particularly her self-portraits, which still draw huge crowds. Frida herself has become even more popular than her paintings, for proving that women can do anything they want to do, despite obstacles. She is admired for her creativity, her bravery and for following her heart.

# BEATRIX POTTER

**Author and illustrator who created Peter Rabbit**

## PAINTING PETS

Helen Beatrix Potter was born in 1866 into a wealthy family in London, England. Her artistic parents, Rupert and Helen, encouraged Beatrix and her younger brother, Bertram, to draw and paint their many pets. They had rabbits, lizards, mice, hedgehogs, tortoises, snakes, frogs and even a bat! Although they lived in London, the family also spent a lot of time in the north of England and Scotland, and they all loved the countryside.

Beatrix's father realised that she had a special talent for drawing and painting when she was very young. He took her on trips to museums and galleries and introduced her to his artist friends. By the time she was eight, she had filled stacks of notebooks with her drawings. Although she had an art teacher, Beatrix mostly taught herself to paint, copying from paintings in books and exhibitions.

Helen Beatrix Potter

Beatrix with her pet rabbit, Benjamin Bounder

> 66 Thank goodness I was never sent to school; it would have rubbed off some of the originality. 99

As a teenager, her favourite pets were two rabbits, Benjamin Bounder and Peter Piper, who followed her around on leads and did clever tricks. Many of her early paintings were of these two beloved bunnies. Beatrix also created incredibly accurate paintings of plants, and she especially loved to draw scenes from her favourite childhood stories, such as *Cinderella*.

## A RABBIT CALLED PETER

One of her first stories was about a mischievous bunny called Peter Rabbit. She wrote the tale for a little boy called Noel, who was the son of her favourite former governess, Annie Moore. She tried to get it published many times, but no one wanted to make her story into a book.

> **"There is something delicious about writing the first words of a story. You never quite know where they'll take you."**

So Beatrix published it herself, to give to family and friends. When they saw the finished book, the publisher Frederick Warne changed their minds and asked her to illustrate it in colour. She did, and it was an instant success, so she quickly went on to create more books about Peter Rabbit and his friends. Beatrix fell in love with her editor, Norman Warne, but just after they became engaged he suddenly died of leukaemia. Beatrix was heartbroken.

But she found great happiness in nature, especially in the Lake District. She eventually wrote and illustrated 28 books and designed the first-ever Peter Rabbit toy, as well as Peter Rabbit tea sets, slippers and a board game. The world's favourite bunny was also the first character from a children's story to become a brand beyond the book.

Passionate about protecting nature, Beatrix eventually bought 15 farms around the Lake District. Her favourite farm was called Hill Top and it became the setting for many of her books. Working closely with the National Trust, she helped to stop people who wanted to buy and build on the beautiful wilderness land. During this time, she married William Heelis, a solicitor whom she met through her environmental work, and they lived happily together for many years. Not only did she help preserve nature, she also helped to improve the lives of people living near her home, bringing more nurses to the area. She loved to work on her farms, wearing muddy clogs and a shawl and helping with the haymaking and sheep. Beatrix Potter died in 1943, leaving over 4,000 acres of land to the National Trust.

> **"We cannot stay home all our lives, we must present ourselves to the world and we must look upon it as an adventure."**

## SHAKING THE WORLD

Beatrix is one of the world's best-loved children's authors and illustrators, and her timeless creations have entertained and delighted millions of children for over a hundred years. Not only talented but generous as well, Beatrix worked hard to save the beautiful natural world she loved.

Over two million copies of her books are sold every year — that's around four books every minute. Making children's book illustration into a respectable and desirable career, her work paved the way for countless authors, illustrators and stories to come, as the world saw how successful children's books could be — and how incredibly important they were.

Some of Beatrix's most famous books including *The Tale of Peter Rabbit*

# COCO CHANEL

## INVENTIVE ORPHAN

The second of six children, Gabrielle Bonheur Chanel was born in Saumur, France, in 1883. Her mother, who worked in a laundry, died when Gabrielle was young, and her father, a travelling salesman, put her into an orphanage so she could be cared for by the nuns there. The nuns did a very important thing for Gabrielle: they taught her how to sew, embroider and iron at an early age. She lived with them until she was 18, when she left for Paris to start a new life.

She got the nickname, 'Coco', as a singer on stage. But she soon decided that singing was not the job for her, and started a hat-making business instead. She opened her first shop in 1910, with money from one of her friends and admirers, and as her business became more successful, she started making and selling clothes as well. Within six years, Coco's shops were doing so well that she was able to repay all the money she had borrowed.

## CHIC AND COMFORTABLE

One of Coco's first successful fashion designs was an old jumper that she turned into a dress one chilly day. Whenever someone admired her dress, she offered to make one for them. This example of making something comfortable into something stylish was at the heart of how she approached fashion: in a time when women were still wearing tight corsets and long petticoats, she set them free. Daringly, she shortened hemlines on skirts and dresses, and designed trousers so that women could walk faster, ride bicycles and do all the things that men could do.

**"In order to be irreplaceable one must always be different."**

Coco was glamorous, and people wanted to copy her look. She wore her hair very short, in the 'boyish' style that was becoming popular in the 1920s. She also created a perfume, and gave it a number because she was told by a fortune teller it was her lucky number: Chanel Number 5 was the first fragrance to carry a designer's name and became the best-selling perfume of all time.

It is still popular today, and so are many of her designs such as her Little Black Dress and her famous jacket-and-skirt suits. With the Little Black Dress, Coco took a colour that was normally used for mourning, and showed the world how chic and practical it could be. Her first suit design, which boldly borrowed from men's fashion in a way no one had done before, was comfortable and elegant at the same time.

**"Luxury must be comfortable, otherwise it is not luxury."**

Throughout the 1920s, Coco's business grew and grew. She was popular in the world of literature and art, too, designing costumes for ballets and spending time with her artist friends such as Pablo Picasso. In the 1930s, Coco's business continued to do well, even when financial problems all over the world meant that people weren't spending much money on fashion. But when the Second World War broke out, she closed her shops and let her staff go, eventually moving to Switzerland.

The bottle of Coco's first perfume, Chanel No. 5, looks almost exactly the same now as it did in the 1920s

Coco with her dog, Gigot

Then, when she was 70 years old, Coco came back to Paris, saying she was "dying of boredom". Once again, she became a leader in the world of fashion, winning over women with her elegant, easy-to-wear designs.

## SHAKING THE WORLD

Many books have been written, and an award-winning musical and a film have been made about Coco, because the story of the designer herself is as fascinating as the clothes she created. She changed the world of fashion forever, freeing women from clothing that restricted them. Many of her designs, combining style and comfort, and her perfume, are as popular today as they were nearly 100 years ago.

Gabrielle Bonheur 'Coco' Chanel

" The most courageous act is still to think for yourself. Aloud. "

# BILLIE HOLIDAY

One of the greatest jazz singers of all time

## POVERTY AND PROBLEMS

Billie Holiday, whose real name was Eleanora Fagan, was born in 1915 in Philadelphia, USA, to a teenage mother, Sadie. Her father is believed to be Clarence Holiday, who later became a successful jazz musician, but Eleanora almost never saw him. Her early life was incredibly tough, and she grew up in extreme poverty. She once said: "I never had a chance to play with dolls like other kids. I started working when I was six years old."

Billie with her trademark gardenias in her hair

Sadie and Eleanora moved to Baltimore. Her mother had to go to court because Eleanora had skipped so much school, and Eleanora was sent to a special home for African-American girls with problems. She was just nine, one of the youngest girls there.

Nickname: Lady Day

**"If I'm going to sing like someone else, then I don't need to sing at all."**

If Eleanora had problems, music was her way out. Baltimore had a big jazz scene in the 1920s, and she soaked up the music. She was never formally trained, but she started singing along to records by famous jazz singers like Louis Armstrong or Bessie Smith. Eleanora changed her name to Billie, after a popular film star. When Billie was 15, she and Sadie moved to New York City, and Billie Holiday made her debut in the nightclubs of Harlem. When she was 18, she got the chance to sing with a well-known band.

## SUCCESS ... AND SADNESS

From then on, Billie's life began to change. She started recording songs that became a big part of early American jazz music and are still popular today. She recorded one of her greatest hits, 'What a Little Moonlight Can Do', in 1935 when she was just 20 years old, and the next year she recorded 'Summertime', from the musical *Porgy and Bess*. She worked with many of the most famous jazz musicians: Lester Young, Count Basie and then, in 1938, she sang with Artie Shaw, becoming the first black woman to sing with a white orchestra.

Billie often performed at places where African Americans were not allowed, other than on stage. Around that time, she discovered the poem 'Strange Fruit', which was about a black man being killed by white people. She first sang the song in public at Café Society, New York's first nightclub where people of different races enjoyed music together. 'Strange Fruit' was the first song to protest against racism, and it changed popular music forever.

At Café Society, Billie started singing with her head tilted back and white flowers called gardenias in her hair — a look that soon became as famous as Billie herself. More importantly, though, her music changed as she started singing more emotional, powerful, soulful songs. In 1941, she recorded 'God Bless the Child', which was inspired by the poverty and hard times of her childhood. Her mother died in 1945, and Billie was broken-hearted.

**" If I don't have friends, then I ain't got nothing. "**

Billie with jazz musician Louis Armstrong

Although her singing career was very successful, Billie was also deeply unhappy and lonely. She turned to drugs and alcohol to make herself feel better — but only succeeded in making her problems much, much worse. Between 1952 and 1959, she made 100 new recordings, sang to sold-out crowds at Carnegie Hall in New York City, won many awards and toured Europe . . . but none of this gave her the happiness she longed for.

**" Sometimes it's worse to win a fight than to lose. "**

## SHAKING THE WORLD

Billie died tragically young, at just 44, overcome by her unhappiness. She was a musical genius who had never even learned to read music, a star with the world at her feet who felt empty and lost. But her sadness was part of what made her singing so beautiful: she had a deeply soulful style, with a precise, rich way of phrasing her words, full of feeling and incredibly powerful. She left the world too soon, but she left behind her music, songs that many believe made her the best jazz singer of all time.

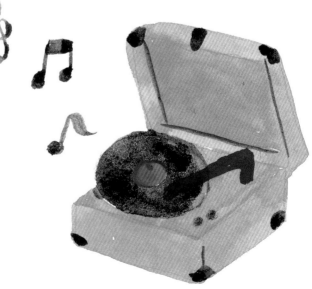

# ANNA PAVLOVA

**The most celebrated ballerina in the world**

## DREAMS OF DANCING

Anna Pavlovna Pavlova was born in 1881 during the cold, icy winter in St Petersburg, Russia. Her father died when she was just two years old, and her mother worked as a laundress so that she could buy food for her young daughter. Life was not easy. But one magical night, her mother managed to get tickets for the ballet . . . and Anna's life changed forever. She fell in love with ballet at first sight, and was determined to grow up to be a ballerina like the ones she had seen leaping and spinning across the stage.

Anna as a young woman

> " *The right to happiness is fundamental.* "

> " *To follow, without halt, one aim: There's the secret of success.* "

Russia had — and still has — some of the best ballet schools in the world. Eight-year-old Anna had her mind set on getting a place at one of them, even if it meant having to move away from her mother. She went for an audition to try to prove that she was born to dance, but she did not get in, because she was too young. Two years later, she tried again and was offered a place at the Imperial Ballet School. Her dream was beginning to come true.

Anna worked very hard. She was taller and thinner than the other girls, and some of them teased her, calling her a 'broom'. Though Anna was not as strong as some of the other dancers, she did not let this stop her. She worked out how to make her ballet shoes stronger so that she could dance on the tips of her toes more easily. When Anna danced, her whole body trembled because her muscles had to work so hard. But as she grew older and kept practising, she created a style of dance all her own.

## THE SWAN

At the time, ballet was much sportier and more acrobatic than the style of dance we know today. Anna's graceful, delicate movements — which trembled with feeling and brought stories to life — were dramatic and beautiful, and set her apart from other dancers.

Anna performing 'The Dying Swan' ballet

Anna grew more and more famous, dancing the lead part in all the ballets. Her best-known solo, and the most loved by her many fans, was called 'The Dying Swan'.

Anna danced her way across Europe and, eventually, the rest of the world, travelling to places where people had never seen ballet before. She believed that everyone should know about ballet, no matter how poor or how far away they were. She studied dance in countries from India to Spain, learning from the performers there and adding to her amazing power as a dancer.

Anna never forgot where she came from. In Paris, France, she started an orphanage for young Russian refugees, caring for them as if they were the children she had never had. She also loved animals, especially swans, and had a lake built at her London home, filled with the graceful creatures that inspired her dancing.

One winter's night, a train Anna was travelling on crashed. When she wandered outside into the snow in her pyjamas to find out what was happening, she caught a terrible cold that turned into pneumonia. As she lay dying, she called for her dress made of feathers, perhaps dreaming that she was going on stage for a final dance as a swan.

Anna in her garden with her pet swans

> **No one can arrive from being talented alone, work transforms talent into genius.**

## SHAKING THE WORLD

Anna changed the world of dance forever, bringing a new kind of magic and poetry to ballet. Loved around the world for her warmth and her ability to reach out and inspire others, Anna made ballet into an art form for everyone, showing the world that grace and beauty belong to all of us.

# MIRABAI

## A SPECIAL GIFT

Mira was born in Rajasthan, in northern India, in the early 16th century. When she was three years old, a wandering religious man called a 'sadhu' came to her home and gave little Mira a doll of Sri Krishna, who is believed by Hindus to be a descendant of God. Her father did not want her to have it because he didn't think she would be able to appreciate the special gift, but Mira loved the little doll and refused to eat anything until her father gave it to her! She decided then and there to follow Sri Krishna and to love him for the rest of her life.

A modern-day poster of Mirabai

> **66** Don't forget love; it will bring all the madness you need. **99**

## SAINTS AND SONGS

One day, when Mira was a bit older, she saw a wedding procession and asked, "Who will be my husband?" Her mother joked with her, saying, "You already have a husband: Sri Krishna!" She knew how much Mira loved the holy Hindu figure and encouraged Mira's beliefs. Sadly, though, Mira's mother died when she was very young.

When she grew up, Mira's father arranged a marriage for her, according to tradition. She was married to Prince Bhoj Raj and, even though her husband's family was wealthy and powerful, Mira was not happy in her new life. She continued to worship and sing to Sri Krishna, even though her husband's family did not like it. The family became very jealous of Mira, who had become famous for her faith and her singing, but Mira continued to worship her beloved Sri Krishna.

Mira's temple to Krishna in Rajasthan, India

Her poems, which were songs called *bhajans*, became more and more well-known and soon people were singing them all over the north of India. Then her fame drew the attention of the Emperor Akbar, who was a Muslim and an enemy of Mira's husband's family.

> **66** Without the energy that lifts mountains, how am I to live? **99**

36

Akbar was determined to meet the 'princess-saint', as she was called, so he disguised himself as a poor beggar, came to her home, and gave her a beautiful jewelled necklace as a sign of his admiration.

> **"The heat of midnight tears will bring you to God."**

Also known as Meera Bai or Mira Bai

When Mira's jealous husband found out, he was very angry and commanded her to kill herself! As she obediently walked into the river to drown, she had a vision of Sri Krishna, who told her to go instead to a place called Brindaban and continue to worship him — so Mira did.

Finally, her husband, who felt very guilty for his anger, begged her to return home, so Mira did. Soon after, her husband died and his family blamed her for his death, commanding her to commit *suttee*, an ancient tradition where the wife was expected to throw herself on to her husband's funeral pyre and die in the flames . . . But Mira refused. She said that her real husband was Sri Krishna, who had not died.

Her husband's family continued trying to make her life miserable, stopping her going out and even trying to kill her! Finally, she escaped from the palace and went back to Brindaban, where she could worship freely.

When she died, it is said that Sri Krishna came to the temple where she was worshipping and opened his heart centre to her, and she left her body and melted into the heart of her beloved.

A statue of Mirabai, now celebrated as a saint in Northern India

## SHAKING THE WORLD

Mira wrote many *bhajans* that are still sung today and has inspired millions of people with her devotion to Sri Krishna. Even though she was born a princess, she turned her back on wealth and luxury and lived as a beggar in the streets, because all that mattered to her was her love of Sri Krishna. Although she suffered for her beliefs, her faith transformed her life into one of love and joy.

# MAYA ANGELOU

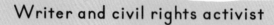

A young Maya (top) and her book, *I Know Why the Caged Bird Sings* (bottom)

## CAGED BIRD

Marguerite Annie Johnson was born in 1928 in St Louis, Missouri, USA. After her parents separated, she and her brother, Bailey, were sent to live with their grandmother in the town of Stamps, Arkansas. Bailey couldn't pronounce Marguerite, so he called her Maya . . . and the nickname stuck. Then a terrible thing happened. When Maya was seven and the children were home visiting their mother, Maya was viciously attacked by her mother's boyfriend. She was so shocked and hurt by what happened that she stopped speaking for five years.

Back in Stamps, her grandmother's friend, Mrs Flowers, introduced Maya to books and taught Maya that some books needed to be read aloud — and Maya slowly found her voice again. Maya was a brilliant child and did well in school. Books and words became her safe place, where she felt happy and free.

Maya Angelou

## FROM SILENCE TO SONG

When she was a teenager, Maya moved to San Francisco, where she earned a scholarship to study dance and acting. She became the first woman and the first African American to work as a tram conductor. After she had a baby boy, Guy, she did all sorts of jobs to support herself and her son, working as a dancer, a cook and a car mechanic. She then married a Greek sailor named Anastasios Angelopulos, and used his name to create her professional name: Maya Angelou.

During the 1950s, Maya was a successful performer, appearing in the famous opera *Porgy and Bess* and many other stage productions. But she poured even more of her energy into her work as a civil rights activist, working for equal treatment for African Americans as well as trying to stop violence against women. Despite her successful career as an actor in the USA, Maya moved abroad in the 1960s, first to Egypt and then to Ghana, before returning to America.

**“My mission in life is not merely to survive, but to thrive.”**

Maya continued to write, but it was not until her friend, the novelist James Baldwin, encouraged her to tell the story of her life that Maya began to change history. In 1969, her memoir about her childhood and teenage years, *I Know Why the Caged Bird Sings*, became the first best-selling non-fiction book written by a female African-American writer.

Maya became an international sensation and went on to write many award-winning plays, scripts, essays, cookbooks, children's books, several volumes of poetry, and five more autobiographical works about her fascinating life. She wrote and recited her poem 'On the Pulse of the Morning' for President Bill Clinton's inauguration. Maya became one of the most successful writers in the world: of her 36 books, 30 were bestsellers.

> **" I know why the caged bird sings. "**

Continually breaking boundaries and taking brave steps into new places, she became Hollywood's first black female screenplay writer. She received 50 honorary degrees and multiple literary and other awards, including an Emmy for her role in the film *Roots*.

Maya's life was always tinged with sadness, though. From the terrible events of her childhood, to the racial abuse she suffered in Arkansas, her journey was not an easy one. When her friend, Dr Martin Luther King, Jr, was killed on her birthday, she stopped celebrating her birthday for many years. But in spite of the sadness, Maya was a survivor, a strong, funny, vibrant woman who surrounded herself with friends, explored the world, and changed many lives with her writing and incredible speaking.

> **" If you don't like something, change it. If you can't change it, change your attitude. "**

Maya was known for her inspirational words

## SHAKING THE WORLD

The little girl who had no voice became one of the most powerful speakers in the world. With rich, deep tones, Maya read her work aloud to packed audiences everywhere. Through her writing and her work, she fought for fair treatment for everyone, exploring African-American history and celebrating women. Writer, actor, screenwriter, dancer, historian, traveller, teacher, trailblazer, poet, friend: Maya was, in the words of her own poem, a 'Phenomenal Woman'.

# GEORGIA O'KEEFFE

A portrait of Georgia
taken in 1930

## INDEPENDENT SPIRIT

Born in 1887, Georgia Totto O'Keeffe was the second of seven children, and grew up on a farm in Wisconsin, USA. Her Irish father was named Francis Calyxtus O'Keeffe, and her Dutch-Hungarian mother was named Ida Totto. Ida had longed to be a doctor and wanted her children to be well educated, encouraging Georgia to take art lessons and to explore nature. Georgia had art in her blood: both her grandmothers and two of her sisters loved to paint, too. She had a strong, independent spirit from an early age, and her parents supported and encouraged her.

## BREAKING BOUNDARIES

After high school, Georgia studied art in Chicago and New York, where she loved discovering the new, modern work of European and American photographers and artists. But after her father's business failed there was no money to pay for her studies, so she started working as an artist and an art teacher instead — and she started to experiment more with her art.

Georgia spent most of her energy trying to find a way to express her ideas. She made a series of abstract charcoal drawings in 1915 — one of the first times an American artist had created abstract works. Abstract art does not try to show something realistically, as it would appear in nature, but instead it uses colours and shapes to express an idea. In Europe, artists such as Pablo Picasso, Wassily Kandinsky and Piet Mondrian were changing the way artists expressed themselves. In the USA, Georgia pushed boundaries with her art, trying her own bold, new way of working.

The art dealer and photographer Alfred Stieglitz saw that her work was special and started showing it to the public. They fell in love and were married a few years later. Georgia spent the 1920s painting skyscrapers and flowers as no one had shown them before: up close, and simplified to their most basic shapes. She quickly became one of the most important artists in the USA. Not only was she a leader in the new art movement, but she was also the only woman at the time to break into this area.

> **"** To create one's world in any of the arts takes courage. **"**

Georgia's 'Jimson Weed' (White Flower No. 1), 1932

In 1929, Georgia's art and life changed forever when she made her first trip to New Mexico. Inspired by the dramatic landscape, the buildings made of dried, red mud blocks, and Native American art, Georgia fell in love with New Mexico and eventually made it her permanent home. She painted the stark, beautiful high desert and the things she saw in it, from cow skulls to clouds, and created some of her best-known paintings there.

**"**I found I could say things with colour and shapes that I couldn't say any other way — things I had no words for.**"**

In 1946, The Museum of Modern Art in New York City held a show of her life's work, the first time they had done this for a female artist. Georgia was at the height of her fame and her creative power, but when Alfred died that same year, she grew restless and she began to travel all over the world. She continued to paint into her old age, even though her eyesight began to fail, creating her last oil painting without help in 1972. At 90, she said, "I can see what I want to paint. The thing that makes you want to create is still there." She continued painting with the help of assistants and her vivid memory and imagination, before she finally died at the age of 98.

Georgia with her painting, 'Horse Skull with White Rose', 1931

## SHAKING THE WORLD

Georgia changed art forever with her groundbreaking style. Her artwork was completely different to what everyone else was doing: it was her own distinctive, bold and beautiful way of interpreting the world around her. Her thousands of paintings inspired new generations of artists to push creative boundaries, and opened up the art world for all the women who came after her.

**"**I've been absolutely terrified every moment of my life — and I've never let it keep me from doing a single thing I wanted to do.**"**

Georgia Totto O'Keeffe

# EMILY BRONTË

## LOVE AND LOSS

Emily Jane Brontë was born in 1818 in the village of Thornton, in Yorkshire, England. She was the fifth child of Maria Branwell Brontë and the Reverend Patrick Brontë, an Irish clergyman and writer. Their six children — Maria, Elizabeth, Charlotte, Branwell, Emily and Anne — inherited Patrick's rich imagination and love of storytelling, but their childhoods were very sad.

When Emily was three, the family moved to Haworth, also in Yorkshire. Sadly, her mother, Maria, died of cancer a few months later. Although an aunt came to look after the children, she was often busy, so the young Brontës turned to their clever, kind eldest sister for comfort instead. Seven-year-old Maria read to them from newspapers and organised games. But just a few years later, both Maria and their next-eldest sister Elizabeth caught tuberculosis, and died six weeks apart.

Without their adored older sisters, the four youngest Brontës became closer. They had no friends in the village, but with their vivid imaginations, they were never bored. Emily went to school for just nine months of her life, but she was very clever and learned quickly at home, where her father encouraged all his children to read constantly.

> **If I could I would always work in silence and obscurity, and let my efforts be known by their results.**

Emily started writing as soon as she learned to read. She and her siblings invented imaginary worlds called Angria and Gondal, writing stories and poems about them, and living in them as if they were real. Surrounded by the bleak, lonely Yorkshire moors, the four children saw little of the outside world, but became incredibly good at creating stories to entertain themselves.

The only known portrait of Emily (right), with her sister, Anne, from a group portrait by her brother, Branwell

> **Honest people don't hide their deeds.**

Emily Jane Brontë

# INCREDIBLE IMAGINATION

Patrick Brontë wanted his daughters to become governesses, but the three sisters were destined to become writers instead. When they realised they had all secretly been writing poetry, they joined together to have their poems published. Because women in those days did not usually write, they used male pen names: Acton, Currer and Ellis Bell, each taking the name that matched her initials. The sisters spent £50 (around £5,000 in today's money) publishing it, but the book sold only two copies. Critics today agree that only Emily showed real poetic talent — perhaps even genius.

> **" I am now quite cured of living in society . . . a sensible man ought to find sufficient company in himself. "**

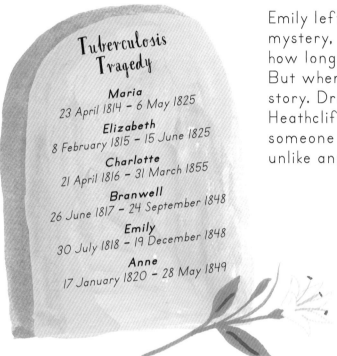

**Tuberculosis Tragedy**

**Maria**
23 April 1814 – 6 May 1825

**Elizabeth**
8 February 1815 – 15 June 1825

**Charlotte**
21 April 1816 – 31 March 1855

**Branwell**
26 June 1817 – 24 September 1848

**Emily**
30 July 1818 – 19 December 1848

**Anne**
17 January 1820 – 28 May 1849

Emily left few letters or diaries, so she herself was a bit of a mystery, and her writing was mysterious as well. No one knows how long she spent working on her first and only published novel. But wherever it came from, *Wuthering Heights* was an incredible story. Dramatic and poetic, it tells the tale of stormy, troubled Heathcliff, who falls hopelessly in love with a woman who marries someone else. Emily's novel was serious, powerful, tragic — and unlike anything that had come before.

But readers weren't ready for such a brave, dark novel, and it was not successful — unlike her sisters' novels, which were published at the same time. Charlotte's *Jane Eyre* was an immediate sensation, but Emily never got to see her own novel's later success. *Wuthering Heights* is now known as one of the greatest novels ever written, but Emily — who had been suffering from tuberculosis for a long time — never published another word and died when she was just 30 years old.

## SHAKING THE WORLD

Even though Emily had no friends outside the family, she had an amazing gift for creating unique characters with deep feelings and dramatic lives. Her incredible imagination transformed her lonely world into a rich and wonderful place — and made her into one of the greatest English writers who ever lived. It is fascinating to wonder what else Emily and her brilliantly talented siblings might have accomplished if they had not all died of acute tuberculosis, which the Victorians called 'consumption'. They all died tragically young, and their brilliant minds and talents were indeed consumed by the devastating disease. How many more masterpieces might they have created, had they lived?

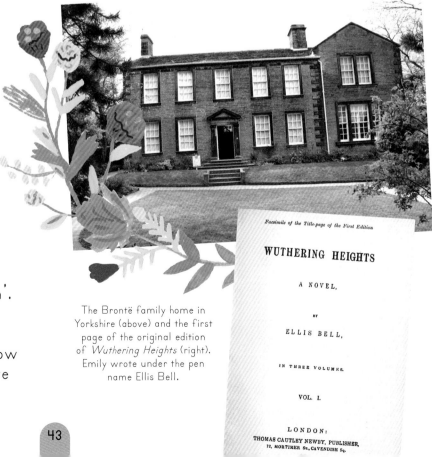

The Brontë family home in Yorkshire (above) and the first page of the original edition of *Wuthering Heights* (right). Emily wrote under the pen name Ellis Bell.

*Facsimile of the Title-page of the First Edition*

**WUTHERING HEIGHTS**

A NOVEL,

BY

ELLIS BELL,

IN THREE VOLUMES.

VOL. I.

LONDON:
THOMAS CAUTLEY NEWBY, PUBLISHER,
72, MORTIMER St., CAVENDISH Sq.

# SARAH BERNHARDT

## ROCKY START

Sarah Marie Henriette Rosine Bernard was born in Paris, France, in 1844 to a Jewish Dutch woman named Julie Bernard. No one knows who her father was, when her birthdate was or indeed exactly what Sarah's full name was. Julie left her daughter first with a hired nurse, then at boarding school and later at a convent. Sarah was often injured or ill and, with a strong temper, she was often in trouble, too. Once, when she was very young and fell into the fireplace and was burned, her mother came rushing to care for her, but mostly Sarah saw her mother very rarely, and probably felt unwanted and unloved.

Sarah as a young woman

But Sarah was a survivor, with a strong will to match her temper. She loved to collect pets, from spiders and crickets to lizards, blackbirds and goats. She loved the nuns at the convent, too, and wanted to become one. However, she also had a talent for acting. The first time she appeared onstage at boarding school, as the Queen of the Fairies, she was paralysed with fright and burst into tears, but the second time, at the convent, she played the angel Raphael and was a great success. Her mother's friend, the powerful Duke of Morny, encouraged Sarah to become an actress, arranging for her to study at the Paris Conservatoire.

## A STAR IS BORN

Sarah made her debut aged 18 with France's national theatre company but, after slapping another actress, she lost her job and fled to Brussels, Belgium. There, she had a baby, named Maurice, whose father was a prince. When she returned to Paris, she became a huge success. Sarah enchanted audiences with her beauty, her emotional performances and her famous 'golden voice'. She understood how to create a picture onstage with herself at the centre, mesmerising her audiences.

But Sarah was not only a brilliant actress: she had great generosity and enormous practical energy, organising a military hospital at the Odéon during the Franco-Prussian War. After the war, she continued giving wildly popular performances, and became a true international star. Travelling everywhere from Australia to South America, she triumphantly returned to Paris a multi-millionaire.

> " He who is incapable of feeling strong passions, of being shaken by anger, of living in every sense of the word, will never be a good actor. "

Everywhere she went, she captured hearts and broke boundaries. Sarah was one of the first women to play the role of Hamlet. Other male roles included the 21-year-old son of Napoleon . . . when Sarah was 55. When Sarah was a grandmother, she played the 19-year-old Joan of Arc. Her talent was so great that she was convincing in any role.

Sarah knew that audiences adored her, and she gave them what they loved — even when it cost her greatly to do so. After falling during a tour and hurting her knee badly, she continued performing, but it never fully healed and — 10 years later, suffering from gangrene — Sarah had to have her leg amputated.

Sarah dressed as the son of Napoleon in a play about Napoleon II

> **" Life begets life. Energy creates energy. It is by spending oneself that one becomes rich. "**

Refusing to feel sorry for herself, she continued acting with a prosthetic leg, visiting soldiers on the front lines during the First World War and starting her last international tour at the age of 70. Finally, though, Sarah's great energy began to fail. When she died, the actors from her theatre walked through the streets of Paris in full costume to pay their respects at her home. Her funeral was attended by thousands.

## SHAKING THE WORLD

Many people believe Sarah was the greatest actress who ever lived. She had devoted fans all over the globe, becoming one of the world's first international superstars.

> **" The theatre is the involuntary reflex of the ideas of the crowd. "**

With a huge talent and an even bigger personality, she fascinated audiences as much with her life offstage as with her roles onstage, inspiring fashion, art and novels. Famous American author Mark Twain once said that there were five kinds of actresses, "bad actresses, fair actresses, good actresses, great actresses — and then there is Sarah Bernhardt." She was so extraordinary that she was in a league all her own.

Sarah Marie Henriette Rosine Bernhardt

# FLORENCE NIGHTINGALE

The founder of modern nursing

CRIMEA

## CALLED TO HELP

Florence was born in 1820 and named after her birthplace: Florence, in Italy. Her sister was called Parthenope, an old name for Naples. When Florence was one, the family returned to England. Her father William had a large library, and little Florence enjoyed reading. Her mother Frances gave parties for famous artists, writers and politicians.

Florence as a young woman

But Florence didn't like parties, preferring to play alone. Her favourite game was hospital, where she cared for her dolls, writing lists and charts about their illnesses and medicines. When Florence was a teenager and her family visited other countries in Europe, what she noticed most were the poor and the sick. Florence began to believe that she was being called to a 'quest' by God: to become a nurse and take care of people.

Her parents refused, because upper-class young ladies like Florence did not work as nurses in those days. But Florence was determined. She visited an orphanage in Germany and hospitals in Paris, France, writing letters to doctors all over Europe, asking questions and comparing their answers. Then she returned to Germany to train as a nurse.

## HYGIENE AND HEALTH

Florence was soon ready for her first job, becoming the unpaid manager of a London hospital for poor women. She ensured that her nurses washed their hands, which was unusual at that time, and that her patients were washed — another new idea. She gave them hot, nutritious meals, and bells to call for help. The hospital was kept very clean and patients' health improved. Her nurses saw that her ideas worked and they respected Florence.

Then the British government asked Florence to help deal with the terrible conditions for soldiers in the Crimean War in Turkey. She accepted the challenge and, although the doctors were unsure about accepting help from women, they quickly realised they needed Florence. She and her team cleaned the hospital, got supplies like medicine and bandages, and gave better food to the soldiers. Florence carried a lamp around the dark hospital as she checked on her patients each night. The soldiers loved the brave, hardworking nurse, and called her 'The Lady with the Lamp'.

A Turkish lamp just like Florence might have used during the Crimean War

**"Nursing is an art."**

After the war, Florence was a hero. She returned to England to continue fighting her own war against dirt and disease. People gave money to her Nightingale Fund, which paid for her work improving hospitals and taught the public about the importance of caring for the poor.

Known as 'The Lady with the Lamp'

> **"I attribute my success to this: I never gave or took any excuse."**

Florence used facts and numbers in her many reports about the changes needed in healthcare, inventing the pie chart, which is now a common way to show number facts. She also started the Florence Nightingale Training School for nurses in 1860, changing people's ideas about nursing and making it a respectable profession for women. Nightingale nurses began setting up training centres around the world.

Florence herself met Queen Victoria many times, sharing her ideas about improving care for hospital patients. Her biggest idea was that illness could be prevented with good hygiene, and that better food, cleanliness and care could stop illness in the first place. The notion of preventive care was a radical one, and many people did not believe her.

Florence with a class of nurses at St Thomas' Hospital, London, 1886

> **"Were there none who were discontented with what they have, the world would never reach anything better."**

## SHAKING THE WORLD

Florence never gave up trying. Even though she spent much of the rest of her life ill in bed, Florence continued to work tirelessly, writing over 13,000 letters as she tried to change people's ideas about the connection between cleanliness and good health. Florence was the inspiration for the founding of the International Red Cross, and won many important awards for her work. Florence died in 1910, at the age of 90, having dedicated her life to helping the sick and the poor. Far ahead of her time, she had changed people's ideas about health and hospitals, creating the modern profession of nursing and transforming medical care not just in Britain, but around the world.

Florence's book, *Notes on Nursing* was first published in 1859, and is still used all over the world today

# HELEN KELLER

Writer and activist who overcame her disabilities to help others

## DARK DAYS

Helen Adams Keller was born in 1880 in Alabama, USA. Her parents, Kate Adams Keller and Colonel Arthur Keller, adored their bright baby daughter, who started talking aged just six months. But when she was 19 months old, Helen fell ill with what the doctor called a 'brain fever'. No one knows exactly what caused it — perhaps scarlet fever or meningitis — but the result was that Helen was now both completely blind and profoundly deaf.

Helen as a young girl (top). As well as learning Braille, Helen learned to write in very square block letters using a ruler as a guide (bottom).

> **Alone we can do so little; together we can do so much.**

With the help of the cook's daughter, Martha Washington, Helen invented her own form of sign language, but she was unable to interact with anyone else. As Helen grew older, she became wild and angry, almost completely locked inside herself. Everyone suggested to Helen's parents that she be sent to an institution. Desperate to help her daughter, Helen's mother Kate investigated tirelessly, determined to find a better solution.

At the Perkins Institute for the Blind in Boston, the Kellers met a teacher named Annie Sullivan, and hired her to help rescue Helen from her dark, lonely world. By now, Helen was six years old. But things got worse after Annie's arrival. Annie tried to teach Helen 'finger spelling', forming the letters on Helen's hand as she touched an object. And although she was curious at first, Helen's tantrums increased as she grew more and more frustrated.

> **Although the world is full of suffering, it is also full of the overcoming of it.**

Helen Adams Keller

## WATER AND WORDS

Then one day Annie took Helen to the water pump to try to teach her the connection between the letters and the water itself. As she pumped water over Helen's hand, she spelled the letters W–A–T–E–R on to Helen's palm — over and over again. Suddenly, it all made sense to Helen! The thing she was feeling had a name. She grabbed Annie and ran everywhere, asking Annie to teach her the 'letter names'. By bedtime that night, she had learned 30 new words.

This is an example of the British deafblind block alphabet

Helen graduating from Radcliffe College

After this breakthrough, Helen learned quickly. A few years later, Annie went with Helen to the Horace Mann School for the Deaf, then on to the Perkins School for the Blind. Using finger-spelling, lip-reading and Braille, Helen became a strong student. At all her schools, Annie went to Helen's classes with her, translating the teachers' words into Helen's palm. Helen still struggled to speak, though; few but Annie could understand her. But Helen persisted and at Radcliffe College (now part of Harvard University), she became the first deaf-blind person ever to earn a degree from college or university, graduating with high honours.

Helen wanted to help other deaf and blind people, and to make the world understand how disabled people felt. With the help of John Macy, she wrote her autobiography, called *The Story of My Life*, which was published before she graduated. Overcoming her speaking difficulties while still depending on Annie for help, Helen began talking to audiences all around the USA and eventually, all around the world. She made a Hollywood film about blindness, and wrote articles, essays and four more books. As an adviser for the newly organised American Foundation for the Blind, she helped raised large amounts of money as well as raising awareness about disability.

> 66 The best and most beautiful things in the world cannot be seen or even touched — they must be felt with the heart. 99

## SHAKING THE WORLD

Helen changed the way the world saw blind and deaf people — and she changed the way disabled people were treated, too. Travelling to over 35 countries, she helped educate the world about disability, sharing the message that disabled people are just like everyone else. She helped to start the American Civil Liberties Union, which continues to work to ensure that everyone is treated equally.

Famous from the age of eight, Helen dedicated her life to helping, encouraging and inspiring others to overcome disability. What Helen achieved, through hard work and determination, was truly amazing. With the help of her teacher and friend, Helen proved to the world that courage and persistence can help overcome any challenge, no matter how great.

# ANNIE SULLIVAN

Annie as a young woman

## BLINDNESS AND BRAVERY

Johanna 'Annie' Mansfield Sullivan had a tragic childhood. Born to Irish parents in Massachusetts, USA, in 1866, Annie and her younger siblings — two of whom died as babies — grew up in terrible poverty. When she was five, Annie got a disease called trachoma, which badly damaged her sight. When she was eight, her mother died. Her father abandoned Annie and her little brother Jimmie — both ill — and they were sent to the filthy, crowded poorhouse. Jimmie died soon after, and Annie was heartbroken: without her beloved little brother to care for, she was utterly alone.

Johanna Mansfield Sullivan

When she was 14, Annie finally escaped by bravely pleading for help from a wealthy visitor, who sent her to the Perkins School for the Blind in Boston. Despite eye surgery, she still struggled to see — but that was not her only problem. Because of her difficult childhood and lack of schooling, she struggled to follow rules and didn't know how to behave properly, so she often got into trouble. Annie was extremely clever, though, and graduated top of her class.

## THE MIRACLE WORKER

Because she was an excellent student, when Annie was 20 she was offered a job with the Keller family, to help their deaf-blind daughter Helen. Determined to rescue a wild, frightened child from her dark, silent world, Annie wanted to help Helen understand that things had names. Setting aside all her formal training, she got back to basics, thinking about how children normally learn language.

One day Annie took Helen to the water pump and, as she pumped water over Helen's hand, Annie traced W-A-T-E-R on to Helen's palm — over and over again. Finally, Helen understood! She could now begin to name her world and connect with it. This breakthrough was truly miraculous and, because of it Annie became known as the 'Miracle Worker'.

> "Keep on beginning and failing. Each time you fail, start all over again, and you will grow stronger until you have accomplished a purpose."

> **"Children require guidance and sympathy far more than instruction."**

Annie — whom Helen called 'Teacher' — quickly succeeded in teaching Helen nearly 1,000 words, the times tables and how to read Braille, all in a few months. When Helen was ready to attend Annie's school in Boston, Annie went with her, returning as a hero. Even though Annie still struggled with her own eyesight, which often caused her severe pain, she spent thousands of hours tirelessly spelling lectures and textbooks into Helen's hand. Annie next went with Helen to Radcliffe College, and although she didn't get a degree like Helen did, she helped teach Helen everything she learned there.

While Helen was writing her autobiography with the help of a young Harvard professor called John Macy, Annie and John fell in love. After they were married, Helen went to live with them. Deeply loyal to Helen, Annie's life continued to revolve completely around her former student, as they travelled the world and lectured together. Annie often gave speeches for Helen, since most people still could not understand Helen when she spoke. While she and John grew apart, eventually separating, Annie continued her work at Helen's side for many years. Despite many operations, Annie's own vision worsened, and she needed Helen's help more and more, just as Helen had once leant on Annie for everything. Annie finally lost her sight almost completely before she died at the age of 70.

Annie and Helen remained close friends for 49 years until Annie's death

## SHAKING THE WORLD

Although she struggled with her own sight all her life, Annie saw possibility where everyone else saw only the impossible. She overcame her difficult beginnings as a blind orphan in a poorhouse, to become one of the world's best known and loved educators, as Helen Keller's loyal teacher and friend for 49 years.

> **"People seldom see the halting and painful steps by which the most insignificant success is achieved."**

Without Annie's determination to free Helen from her silent darkness, Helen would have stayed trapped inside herself, unable to see, hear or communicate with the world. Although Annie lived mostly in Helen's shadow, her hard work and dedication gave Helen a full, rich life. Helen knew this, and called Annie "my guardian angel".

# MARY SEACOLE

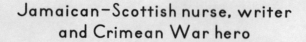

Jamaican–Scottish nurse, writer
and Crimean War hero

## DOCTRESS' DAUGHTER

Mary Jane Grant was born in Kingston, Jamaic, in 1805. Her mother was a free Jamaican woman who ran a boarding house for injured soldiers, and her father was a Scottish soldier. Mary's mother was a traditional healer or 'doctress' who taught her daughter nursing skills, and Mary enjoyed helping her mother and practising on her dolls. She received a good education, both in school and at home.

Mary grew up facing many prejudices because she was mixed-race, in a place where slaves were not freed until 1834. Even though she was free, her life was limited in other ways. But Mary was an optimist, and saw the benefits of her dual heritage: she believed she had inherited her energy and ambition from her Scottish father, and her healing skills from her Jamaican mother. From a young age, she knew that she was going to live a remarkable life.

### MOTHER SEACOLE

When Mary grew up, she continued — along with her sister, Louisa — to manage the family business. She loved to travel and she visited many places in the Caribbean, Central America and Britain. She also spent time in Panama, using her nursing skills to help fight a terrible cholera epidemic. When things settled down, she managed a hotel that her brother had opened there. She knew a lot about traditional medicine and combined these ideas with more 'modern' European medicine. She believed that cleanliness, good food and fresh air were all an important part of good health — and these were radical ideas at the time.

Her reputation as a healer grew: she helped stop a cholera epidemic in Jamaica, as well as a yellow fever outbreak, and began to treat knife and gunshot wounds. During this time, she had married a naval officer named Edwin Horatio Seacole, but sadly he died after just eight years.

Mary Jane Grant Seacole

> **" ... and the grateful words and smile which rewarded me for binding up a wound or giving a cooling drink was a pleasure worth risking life for at any time. "**

She travelled to England once more in 1854, just after the start of the Crimean War, and asked the War Office to be sent to the Crimea as a nurse. Mary knew she could help, because the greatest danger facing the soldiers was not injury but illness: cholera and malaria were killing far more men than wounds from battle. But the War Office refused Mary's application for the job, possibly because of the colour of her skin.

Mary was clever and resourceful, though, and she wanted to help. So she travelled to the Crimea and used her own money to set up a boarding house called the British Hotel. The hotel had an officers' club and a canteen serving good food, but its main purpose was to take care of sick and wounded officers as they recovered. She often bravely went on to the battlefield to tend to the soldiers there, sometimes under enemy fire. She loaded up mules with supplies, making sure the soldiers had food and blankets, and she always had a kind word for them. The soldiers loved her and called her 'Mother Seacole'. Even though she was praised highly by the soldiers, the military never officially thanked her for her work.

After the war, Mary returned to England, without a penny to her name: she had spent everything she had on helping the soldiers. Luckily, when people heard her story, a festival was organised to raise money to help Mary. She then wrote her memoirs, called *The Wonderful Adventures of Mrs Seacole in Many Lands*. The book was a bestseller, and Mary was able to live comfortably in London for the rest of her life.

Mary's memoir *The Wonderful Adventures of Mrs Seacole in Many Lands*

## SHAKING THE WORLD

Mary did many things that other women did not or could not do during Victorian times: she travelled all over the world, she ran a business and she risked her life to help others. In 2016, a statue of Mary was put up in front of St Thomas' Hospital in London, which is believed to be the first statue of a named black-British woman. It is a richly deserved tribute to someone as courageous, daring and incredibly generous as Mother Seacole.

The only known photograph of Mary, taken in 1873

# SHIRIN EBADI

Iranian human rights lawyer, teacher and activist

## A FAIR AND FEMINIST FATHER

Shirin was born in 1947 in the ancient city of Hamadan, in central Iran, before moving to the capital city, Tehran. Her father, Mohammad Ali Ebadi, was a law professor who wrote several books, while her mother looked after Shirin, her two sisters and her brother, who all grew up surrounded by love and affection.

Mohammad was a feminist, teaching his children that boys and girls are equal. He also taught his children to respect all religions, however, his values of respect, equality and fairness were soon to become a rare thing in Iran.

Shirin on the day she graduated from law school, aged 22

## FROM SHAHS TO SHARIA

Iran was once called Persia, one of the oldest countries in the world. Ruled by shahs (or kings) for hundreds of years, Iran was a place of learning and culture . . . until it was torn apart by revolution in 1979, and a powerful religious leader called Ayatollah Khomeini took charge. Although nearly everyone in Iran is Muslim, the Ayatollah interpreted Islam and its laws — called 'sharia' — in a very strict way. Anyone who spoke out against the Ayatollah was in danger of being arrested and killed.

> **66** If you can't eliminate injustice, at least tell everyone about it. **99**

Aged 30, Shirin had become the youngest and one of the first female judges in Iran, but when the Ayatollah took power, all female judges lost their jobs. Shirin soon realised, though, that her most important work was only just beginning. She wrote many articles and books while raising and educating her two daughters, and continued to teach human rights classes at the University of Tehran. A human right is any right that belongs to all people, especially the right to life, to freedom and to speaking without fear of punishment.

Many people escaped from Iran, fleeing to Europe or the United States. But Shirin stayed. Patiently, she worked and she waited . . . for 22 years.

> **66** My fight is to make sure that only good things happen to my people. **99**

Finally, not long after the Ayatollah's death, she was allowed to practise law again. Working from home, Shirin earned no money from any of the 6,000 people she and her team helped, although one grateful mother tried to pay her with limes. Shirin fought for justice for women, for children and for all whose right to life and freedom was threatened by the Iranian government, becoming a voice for those who have been silenced.

Shirin Ebadi

But the government heard her voice, too, and Shirin was arrested and thrown into prison. After spending 25 days in solitary confinement, Shirin's childhood stammer came back for a time. But once freed, she continued to fight for justice — despite her husband and sister being arrested and many threats against her life.

Shirin was awarded the Nobel Peace Prize in 2003, for her brave work helping to protect women and children in Iran. The first Iranian and the first Muslim woman to win, she used the prize money to set up a new office to continue her work helping others, and to start the Centre for Defenders of Human Rights. Since 2009, she has lived in exile in London, England, not because she is afraid but because outside Iran she has the freedom to try to help the helpless people in her homeland.

> "It's not just about hope and ideas. It's about action."

Shirin with her book, *Until We Are Free*

## SHAKING THE WORLD

Risking her life every day to fight for the human rights of those unable to defend themselves, Shirin has helped countless people. A practising Muslim, she believes Islam can be a religion of peace and justice. She dreams that Iran will one day be a Muslim country guided by Islamic values, as well as a democracy that respects everyone's human rights.

Shirin is hopeful for Iran's future, but she knows that hard work and brave action are needed to help turn Iran into a peaceful nation once more, where learning is valued and where her people no longer live in fear. She knows that Iranian people must continue fighting for a better future, as she says in the title of her latest book: *Until We Are Free.*

# MARIA MONTESSORI

Doctor and teacher who put children's needs first

## LOVE OF LEARNING

Maria as a young woman

Maria was born in Italy in 1870, at a time when children, especially girls, were meant to be seen and not heard. Her father, Alessandro, was an accountant, and her mother, Renilde, was well educated and loved reading, encouraging Maria to learn. Even as a young girl, Maria believed that children should be treated well. Once, she overheard a teacher talking about her, and she refused to look at that teacher again: already she believed that children needed to be respected by adults. Maria was very bright, so her parents moved the family to Rome to help her get a better education. They wanted her to become a teacher, the main profession for women at that time, but Maria loved maths and wanted to become an engineer. The more she studied, though, the more she realised she wanted to do something even more unheard of for girls: she wanted to become a doctor.

After overcoming many challenges, she was finally allowed to study medicine at the University of Rome. As the only woman, she was not allowed to attend any dissections of naked bodies with the men, so she had to do all of her practical work alone at night.

## FOLLOW THE CHILD

Maria's hard work and dedication paid off: in 1896, she became the first female doctor in Italy. She cared deeply about women's and children's rights. While working in a clinic for children with learning disabilities and mental illnesses, she noticed that the children, having nothing else to play with, would play with their food. She came to the conclusion that they didn't need medicine to help them, but a better, kinder education including time to play.

> ## " The child who concentrates is immensely happy. "

A girl learns to trace the alphabet at a Montessori school

Maria went on to become the director of a similar clinic for children with learning disabilities and mental illnesses. With kindness and compassion, Maria taught the children so well that they managed to pass a test that was usually given only to children in mainstream schools. She believed that teachers should not judge children, but accept them and help them to learn in a way that was loving and gentle. Every child, she said, was born with potential, and it was the job of adults to help children discover their unique skills and abilities. She also believed that it didn't matter what background children came from: they could all be equal in their intelligence. All of these ideas were very new and different at the time, and Maria had to work hard to start changing people's minds.

> " Never help a child with a task at which he feels he can succeed. "

Maria Tecla Artemisia Montessori

When Maria was asked to open her first mainstream school, she filled the room with child-sized tables and chairs. She discovered that when the children found a task meaningful and interesting, they had an amazing ability to concentrate. She noticed, too, that they loved putting things back where they belonged, and so she fitted open shelves so the children could tidy and take care of their own space. She believed that even the very youngest children deserved to be treated with dignity, and so she taught them how to look after themselves, to wipe their own noses and button their own coats.

> " Early childhood education is the key to the betterment of society. "

At the end of her first year, Maria renamed her school 'Casa dei Bambini' — the Children's House — and the first Montessori school was born. Maria's first book, *The Montessori Method*, was soon translated into over 20 languages around the world. Her ideas of creating an environment in which children could explore and learn at their own pace, and of encouraging teachers to stand back and 'follow the child', made her a leader in educational thinking all around the world.

## SHAKING THE WORLD

Maria believed strongly in sharing her discoveries, travelling widely to teach others about both mainstream education and education for children with special needs. She was nominated for the Nobel Peace Prize three times before she died aged 81. Her work changed forever the way children were seen and understood, helping teachers all over the world to see things from a child's point of view.

Maria visiting children in one of her schools

# MOTHER TERESA

## Nun and champion of the poor

## FAMILY AND FAITH

Agnes Gonxha Bojaxhiu was born in 1910 in a small town called Skopje, in Albania. She lived with her parents, sister and brother in a large house with a pretty garden. Her family were faithful Catholics, and her mother taught her to love God and other people. Her parents were very kind, generous people, who never turned away someone in need.

When Agnes was just 12, she had a vision that God was calling her to become a nun. She continued with her studies and had to wait six years before she could travel to Ireland, to enter a convent run by the Loreto nuns. She never saw her mother again.

## POOREST OF THE POOR

As a nun, Agnes had to promise to love God above all else, and to commit herself to a life of poverty. She was happy to do this, and after just six months in Ireland, she was sent to India. When she took her vows promising herself to God, she chose a new name, Teresa, after a French saint who believed in doing good by doing 'small things' with joy. In Calcutta, in India, with the Sisters of Loreto, Sister Teresa began her life's work, teaching and caring for the poor.

Agnes as a young woman

But Sister Teresa felt that God was calling her to do more: she needed to get out on to the streets of Calcutta to help the poorest of the poor. After getting special permission from the Pope, she left the Loreto nuns and put on a plain white sari, dressing like the poor women she wanted to help. With just five rupees in her pocket, she started a school in the street, writing on the ground with chalk.

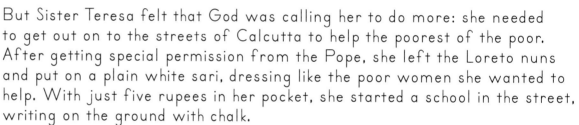

> **"** Poverty is even greater when it is a poverty of the heart. **"**

There were, and there still are, many poor people in Calcutta, and everywhere Sister Teresa looked she saw hunger, disease and suffering. One day, after watching a woman die in the street, she decided to start a home for the dying, where they could live their last days and hours with dignity and peace. At first the work was lonely as well as hard, but it wasn't long before Sister Teresa was joined by other nuns who wanted to help her. The Pope let her start a new order, called the Missionaries of Charity, and she became known as Mother Teresa.

Mother Teresa wanted to help the poor not just to die well, but to live better, so she started opening schools and orphanages in India and all around the world.

58

Agnes Gonxha Bojaxhiu

> ❝ The poor do not need our compassion or our pity; they need our help. What they give to us is more than what we give to them. ❞

> ❝ Let us always meet each other with a smile, for a smile is the beginning of love. ❞

Mother Teresa helping the sick and the poor (above), and a nun working in a hospital in Calcutta, India, set-up by Mother Teresa (left)

There are now over 500 centres in more than 100 countries, helping poor people to have better lives. Leaders from all over the world met with her, and she became a very powerful leader herself, making the world pay attention to the problem of poverty.

## SHAKING THE WORLD

In 1979, Mother Teresa was awarded the Nobel Peace Prize. As with her many other prizes and awards, she gave all the money — including the money that would have been spent on the awards dinner — immediately to the poor. She continued her work for another 20 years, changing millions of lives. She began to have heart trouble in her 80s, but continued working until shortly before her death, helping those less fortunate than herself until her great heart could give no more.

# WANGARI MAATHAI

Environmental and human rights activist

## NATURE LOVER

Wangari Muta Maathai was born in 1940 in a village called Ihithe, in Nyeri, Kenya. As a child, she loved nature, especially walking to the stream to fetch drinking water and watching the tadpoles wriggling in the clear, clean water. Later, her family moved further along the Rift Valley, where her father had found work on a farm, but they soon returned because there weren't enough opportunities for Wangari's education, which was very important to her parents.

Wangari then went to St Cecilia's School, becoming fluent in English and converting to Catholicism. As one of the very best students at the Loreto High School, she was chosen to study in the USA.

## TREES AND TEACHING

In the United States, Wangari earned a degree in biological sciences and a master's degree in science. She went on to became the first woman in East and Central Africa ever to earn a doctorate. She also became chair of the Department of Veterinary Anatomy, and then an associate professor — once again the first woman in this part of Africa to achieve these things.

**❝ Trees are symbols of peace and hope. ❞**

But all these firsts weren't enough for Dr Maathai, who wanted to make an even bigger difference. She listened to local women telling her that streams — like the one she remembered from her childhood — were drying up. Food was less plentiful and they were walking farther and farther to collect firewood. She knew something had to be done to stop the deforestation that was causing so many problems in Kenya. Then she had a brilliant idea.

**❝ To the young people I say, you are a gift to your communities and indeed the world. You are our hope and our future. ❞**

Wangari Muta Maathai

Her idea was that everyone could make a difference in the world, saving the environment one tree at a time. She warned people, "If you destroy the forest, then the river will stop flowing, the rains will become irregular, the crops will fail and you will die of hunger and starvation." Local communities could protect their environment from these problems by planting trees, earning money at the same time. Now called the Green Belt Movement (GBM), Wangari's idea was hugely successful.

Since 1977, the GBM has helped communities plant over 51 million trees in Kenya. It has made the government work harder to protect the environment, stopping farming from destroying the forests, and teaches Kenyans to 'reduce, reuse and recycle'.

Wangari planting a tree with former US president, Barack Obama

Wangari was also passionate about education, which she saw as the answer to ending the HIV/AIDS pandemic that has devastated Africa and left behind nearly 15 million orphans. She believed that the only way to change things and to stop Africa being lost to the threat of disease was "to eliminate ignorance, fear and a sense of helplessness" through education.

**66** We cannot tire or give up. We owe it to the present and future generations of all species to rise up and walk! **99**

Tirelessly working to help protect both her own country and the whole continent of Africa, Wangari wrote four books about ecology and Africa. She also founded the Wangari Maathai Institute for Peace and Environmental Studies, bringing together academic research with the GBM's commuity-led action, so that scientists and villagers can work together to save the Earth. She accomplished all of this while raising three children, Waweru, Wanjira and Muta.

Invited to be a United Nations Messenger of Peace, Wangari addressed the United Nations many times and worked on several international environmental projects, including the Earth Summit. She was awarded many honorary degrees and won dozens of international awards, including the Nobel Peace Prize in 2004, when she became the first African woman to win the prize.

## SHAKING THE WORLD

Wangari dedicated her life to helping women, the environment, Kenya and indeed the rest of Africa, all of which she believed to be linked. A leader in education, she dreamed of a world where communities could be empowered, especially women and children, where the environment could be protected and preserved, and where everyone could live in peace and harmony. Wangari's hard work means that local communities in Kenya — and, thanks to her example, around the world — are many steps closer to achieving that dream.

Wangari demonstrating the success of the Green Belt Movement

# ELIZABETH BLACKWELL

First Anglo-American female doctor

## HAPPY CHILDHOOD

Elizabeth was born in Bristol, England, in 1821. Her parents, Hannah Lane and Samuel Blackwell, were active in the movement to end slavery. Samuel was a gentle, loving father who refused to beat his children, as many parents did back then. Elizabeth and her eight brothers and sisters had very happy childhoods.

A young Elizabeth

When Elizabeth was 11, Samuel moved his family to the United States. Even though his sugar business depended on slave labour, Samuel tried to change the industry and took his family to anti-slavery meetings. The children even refused to eat sugar, in support of the cause of the slaves. Her beloved father died when Elizabeth was 17, but she and her siblings continued his work, even though they no longer had any money.

**❝ It is not easy to be a pioneer — but oh, it is fascinating! ❞**

## HEALING HANDS

Elizabeth became a teacher and set up a school with her sisters because she needed the money and because she loved history. In fact, she found everything to do with the human body disgusting! But then something happened to change her mind — and her life — completely: a close friend, who was dying, said to her that she would not have suffered as much if her doctor had been a woman. In that moment, Elizabeth was inspired to become a doctor. But it was not easy, because no woman had ever done it before in America, nor indeed in most of the world.

The very first record of a female doctor is of Agnodice, who worked in Greece around 350 BC. Dorotea Bucca was a physician in Italy, sometime before 1390. And of course, many thousands of women worked as midwifes and healers, but were not formally trained or recognised as doctors. The medical world was a man's world, and it did not welcome women.

**❝ If society will not admit of woman's free development, then society must be remodelled. ❞**

Dr Elizabeth Blackwell

Elizabeth set about to change that, convincing two doctor friends to help her study. She applied to dozens of medical colleges, and was rejected by all but one: Geneva Medical College in New York. Certain that the male students would never allow a woman to join them, the college let them vote on whether or not she should be admitted. Believing it to be a practical joke, they all voted yes. Although they hadn't taken her seriously, their prank paid off for Elizabeth, who became the first female medical student in the USA.

Elizabeth was the first female doctor to graduate from an American medical school

In 1849, Elizabeth became the first woman to earn a medical degree from an American medical school. She travelled to work in clinics in London, where she became friends with Florence Nightingale, and to Paris, France, where she studied midwifery. In Paris, however, she caught an eye disease from one of her patients that caused her to go blind in one eye, ending her dreams of becoming a surgeon.

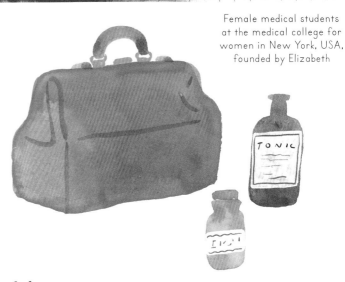

Female medical students at the medical college for women in New York, USA, founded by Elizabeth

Returning to New York City, she set up her own medical practice because no one else would hire a female doctor. Soon, she was joined by her younger sister, Dr Emily Blackwell, and their friend Dr Marie Zakrzewska. Together, they opened The New York Infirmary for Women and Children, which cared for the poor. Ten years later, they opened a medical college for women.

Elizabeth never married, because she wanted to be self-sufficient, but she adopted an Irish orphan named Kitty Berry. Returning with Kitty to England, Elizabeth established a successful medical practice in London, and founded the National Health Society to promote good hygiene, believing that 'prevention is better than cure'. She was far ahead of her time, understanding that simple hand-washing could stop the spread of many diseases.

*"For what is done or learned by one class of women becomes, by virtue of their common womanhood, the property of all women."*

## SHAKING THE WORLD

Elizabeth cared for thousands of women, before, during and after childbirth. She also wrote and published many books, including *Pioneer Work in Opening the Medical Profession to Women*. Elizabeth was indeed a pioneer: shortly after she blazed a trail into the medical world, other women began to join her from all over the USA and Europe. She changed the way people saw women and the medical profession forever.

# EVA PERÓN

## ACCIDENTS AND ACTING

María Eva Duarte was born near Buenos Aires, Argentina, in 1919. Her parents, Juana and Juan, were not married, which embarrassed little Eva. Juan had been wealthy when his older children were born, but Eva only knew tough times. She was a happy child, though, playing outdoors, climbing trees, raising silkworms and dressing up in homemade costumes. The family moved often as Juan looked for work, and then he left them, before dying in a car accident when Eva was six. Her mother moved the children to a bigger city near Buenos Aires, the capital, working as a seamstress to support her family.

Eva as a young woman

> **My biggest fear in life is to be forgotten.**

One day, there was a terrible accident in the house, and Eva was badly burned on her face and arms. Her scars healed, but left her with translucent, glowing skin, which actually made her even more beautiful. Eva loved to recite poetry in school, charming her classmates with her emotional performances. She dreamed of becoming an actress, like the stars in Hollywood films. So, when she was 15, she packed her bags and headed to Buenos Aires. Although she had no training, she quickly got parts in films and plays, and had even more success on the radio, where she soon became famous.

## SAINT EVITA

At a fundraising event to help earthquake victims, Eva met Juan Perón, a colonel in the military. He was much older than her, but they were soon married. Eva helped with her husband's campaign for president. Women did not normally take part in politics, but Eva led the way, founding the Female Peronist Party.

Eva and Juan Perón with their pet dogs

When Perón won, Evita — as her many fans called her — spent much of her time visiting the poor, people in hospital and children in orphanages. She then started the Eva Perón Foundation, where she worked very hard, giving money and medicine to the poor. Those she helped were deeply grateful, and called her *la dama de la esperanza* (the lady of hope). Evita helped build hospitals, schools and homeless shelters, giving away shoes and clothes to the *descamisados*, or 'shirtless ones', who were the poorest workers in Argentina. She also travelled to Europe, giving money to poor children. But some people criticised her for wearing expensive designer clothes and jewels while trying to help people who had nothing.

Evita also believed passionately in women's rights. Giving speeches to huge groups, writing articles and speaking on the radio, she fought hard to help earn women the right to vote and to run for political office — and in 1947, her hard work paid off. Evita continued to work tirelessly for women and for the poor, and was adored by those she helped.

Then, one day, Evita fainted and doctors discovered that she had advanced cancer. She became the first Argentinian to receive chemotherapy. The next year she was nominated as the candidate for vice president, running alongside her husband, but she was too weak and ill to run for office, and had to give up: her political dream would not come true. Evita died a year later, at the age of 33. Millions of Argentinians went to her funeral to honour Evita, who was called 'the Spiritual Leader of the Nation' and considered by many to be a saint. 'Saint Evita' had promised the poor that she cared for them and would not forget them — and they, in turn, did not forget her.

**"When the rich think about the poor, they have poor ideas."**

## SHAKING THE WORLD

Evita became the most powerful woman in all of Latin America. Ruthlessly ambitious, clever and kind, Evita knew how to get what she wanted. She created dreams for people who had none, and they loved her for it. She was glamorous, charismatic and charming, helping to bring Argentina into a more modern era. Passionate about making the world a better place for those who struggled, Evita is still beloved by many as a great champion of the poor and forgotten.

**"Time is my greatest enemy."**

María Eva Duarte de Perón

Eva handing out gifts at the Eva Perón Foundation

65

# MARIE CURIE

Leading scientist and first woman to win a Nobel Prize

## LOSS AND LEARNING

Marie Sklodowska was born in Warsaw, Poland, in 1867. Her mother and father were teachers, and she had four older brothers and sisters: Zosia, Jozef, Bronya and Hela. Like her father, who taught maths and physics, Marie was clever and curious and she did extremely well at school. But then, when she was just 10 years old, her mother died of tuberculosis. Marie and her family were heartbroken.

Marie as a young woman

Marie desperately wanted to go to university, but the university in Warsaw taught only men. In other countries, women were allowed to go, but it was very expensive to study abroad. So Marie and her sister, Bronya, made a promise to each other: they would take turns working to pay for the other to travel abroad to study. Marie worked as a governess and a tutor, saving money so that Bronya could go to university.

Marie Sklodowska Curie

> **"Life is not easy for any of us. But what of that? We must have perseverance and above all confidence in ourselves."**

## REVOLUTIONARY RADIOACTIVITY

When it was her turn, Marie moved to Paris, France, to study at the Sorbonne, a famous university, where she earned a degree in physics, maths and chemistry. Next, she gained a masters degree in physics, and then yet another degree in maths. But life wasn't easy for Marie. She was so poor that she had to live on bread and tea, and she sometimes fainted from hunger. But something lovely happened, too: she met Pierre Curie, a physics professor. They soon fell in love and were married.

Marie worked with her husband to investigate 'radioactivity', a word she came up with to describe how the rays from a rare pure metal called uranium work. She invented the kind of science we now call atomic physics — the study of how substances work in their smallest form, the atom. In 1898, when Marie was 31 years old and had a new baby daughter, Irène, she and Pierre discovered two new pure substances, or elements, called polonium (named after Poland, Marie's home country) and radium. Together, they won the Nobel Prize for their work in physics in 1903. Marie was the first woman ever to win a Nobel Prize.

Marie soon had another baby, Eve. But then her husband, Pierre, was killed when he was knocked down in the street by a carriage, and Marie was devastated. She decided to take over his work, becoming the first ever female professor at the Sorbonne University, and winning another Nobel Prize of her own, this time for chemistry, in 1911.

| 84 | 88 |
|---|---|
| **Po** | **Ra** |
| Polonium | Radium |
| [208.982] | 226.025 |

The two elements discovered by Marie. Polonium was named after her home country, Poland.

During the First World War, Marie realised that soldiers were much more likely to survive if they were operated on quickly. If military doctors had access to x-ray machines, they could make better medical decisions and save more lives. She helped to develop mobile x-ray machines and put them into ambulances that she drove to the front line herself. These machines became known as 'Little Curies' in Marie's honour. She trained doctors and their helpers, teaching them how to use this amazing new life-saving equipment.

Marie in one of the 'Little Curies'

Marie was treated badly by many of the men she worked with and was poorly paid, so she had very little money to live on. Without knowing that they were harmful to her health, she used to carry test tubes full of radioactive materials in her pockets. After spending so much time around the dangerous substances she had discovered and worked with, she grew ill and died.

66 Nothing in life is to be feared, it is only to be understood. Now is the time to understand more, so that we may fear less. 99

## SHAKING THE WORLD

Marie's discoveries of radium and polonium changed science and medicine forever. One of the greatest scientists ever, her work meant that x-ray machines became more useful, and were used more by doctors. They continue to be used today to detect broken bones and other problems, helping doctors to treat and cure their patients. Her daughter Irène also became a scientist and won the Nobel Prize for chemistry in 1935. Thanks to Marie and her amazing family, millions of people have been helped and healed.

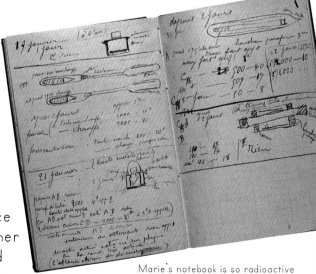

Marie's notebook is so radioactive it is kept in a lead-lined box

66 I was taught that the way of progress was neither swift nor easy. 99

# RACHEL CARSON

Biologist, ecologist and writer who founded the modern environmental movement

## A SENSE OF WONDER

Born in 1907, Rachel was raised on a farm in Pennsylvania, USA, surrounded by the wildlife, woods and wetlands of the Allegheny River. Both her parents, and especially her mother Maria, gave Rachel a deep love of nature from a young age, and inspired in her a sense of wonder about the world around her. Rachel loved writing, too, and won her first prize for a story she wrote when she was 11.

Because she was so good at writing, she planned to study English and become a teacher, but then a professor encouraged Rachel to change her focus to biology — unusual for women at the time. She earned an MA in Zoology and started her PhD, but stopped due to a lack of money during the Great Depression, a time when much of the world suffered from terrible poverty.

Rachel as a young woman

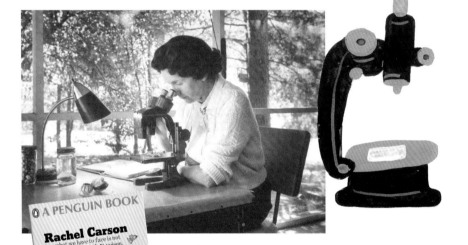

Rachel's book *Silent Spring*, which sparked the modern environmental movement

## PROTECTING THE PLANET

When Rachel's father died, she earned money to support her family, writing radio scripts and magazine articles that combined her love of literature and science. Not long after, her sister died, too, so Rachel began to care for her two nieces, Virginia and Marjorie, while working as an editor and writing award-winning books that combined facts with beautiful, lyrical language.

We are used to thinking about the environment and taking care of the Earth's natural resources, but at the time Rachel was writing, most people believed that controlling nature was the way to make the world a better, more modern place.

From around 1939, farmers had begun using new chemical pesticides to stop insects attacking their crops. Everyone believed that a chemical called DDT was a miracle cure . . . everyone but Rachel. She started warning the public about the dangers of misusing pesticides, reminding people that we are all connected to the Earth. Rachel's idea of how we constantly interact with nature — through what we eat, drink and breathe — was completely new . . . and she started to get a lot of attention.

> **"** But man is a part of nature, and his war against nature is inevitably a war against himself. **"**

Rachel was good at explaining complicated science to ordinary people. Aiming to inspire people to protect the planet, she used simple language, backed up by plenty of facts and statistics, to create a clear call to action.

For many years, Rachel researched the effect of pesticides on the food chain. Then she wrote her most important book yet: *Silent Spring*. When President John F Kennedy learned about her book, he asked scientists to investigate the issues she had raised, and their discoveries proved that Rachel was right.

Rachel speaking out against the use of pesticides

> **"In nature, nothing exists alone."**

Higher amounts of pesticides were found in animals higher up the food chain: the birds — who ate the insects who ate the crops — suffered most. The chemicals the farmers were using were dangerous, and something had to change. Rachel's book had sparked the modern environmental movement.

Big companies that had spent lots of money developing chemical pesticides were furious about these claims and attacked Rachel, calling her a hysterical 'bunny hugger'. But, bravely and calmly, Rachel continued to speak out. By then it was too late to deny what she had uncovered, and the conservation movement grew and grew. Sadly, Rachel did not live to see all the positive changes brought about by her work.

## SHAKING THE WORLD

Rachel taught people to value nature instead of fighting it, to question the use of chemical pesticides, and to treasure the Earth and preserve it for the future. The year after her death, her article 'Help Your Child to Wonder' was re-published as *The Sense of Wonder*, which — along with *Silent Spring* — is considered one of the most important books about nature ever written. Her writing brought about direct change, as new laws were created to protect human health and the natural world. Because of Rachel's work, the world woke up to the urgent need of protecting our fragile planet from its own worst enemy: ourselves.

Rachel Louise Carson

> **"Those who contemplate the beauty of the Earth find reserves of strength that will endure as long as life lasts."**

# ADA LOVELACE

**The world's first computer coder**

## INVENTOR AND DREAMER

Born in 1815, Augusta Ada Byron was the daughter of the famous Romantic poet Lord George Gordon Byron and his wife Lady Anne Isabella Milbanke Byron. But her parents were very unhappily married, and Lady Byron separated from her husband when baby Ada was just a few weeks old. Lord Byron left England months later, never to return, and died in Greece when Ada was just eight years old.

In spite of this sad start, Ada had a fairly happy — if unusual — childhood. Her mother loved mathematics, and believed that it was important for Ada to study maths and science, so that she would not become a wild and moody poet like her father. She also made Ada lie still for hours at a time, to teach her to control her temper. Luckily, Ada was very good at maths and science and languages too, and she enjoyed her studies. Most girls were not taught these subjects because they were thought to be too difficult for them, but Ada proved that this idea was nonsense.

A painting of Ada as a young girl

Young Ada was fascinated by machines and loved to design them herself. The Industrial Revolution was taking place, and steam was being used to power all sorts of wonderful new contraptions. Ada loved reading about them and dreamt up plenty of inventions of her own, from flying machines to whimsical boats.

## CLEVER CODES

Ada was taught by different tutors, from the family doctor to Mary Somerville, who was a Scottish mathematician astronomer and one of the first women allowed into the Royal Astronomical Society. When Ada was 17, she met the inventor Charles Babbage, who saw that Ada was exceptionally intelligent and arranged for her to study advanced maths at the University of London.

A portrait of Ada as a young woman painted in 1840

> **" That brain of mine is something more than merely mortal; as time will show. "**

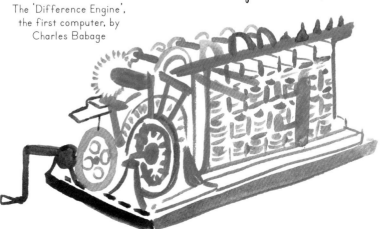

The 'Difference Engine', the first computer, by Charles Babage

Around this time, Ada met a man called William King. They were married and had three children. When William became the Earl of Lovelace, Ada became the Countess of Lovelace. William strongly supported Ada's studies and writing, and they were friends with many of the most interesting people living and working in London, including Charles Dickens.

Ada continued to meet her friend Charles Babbage, because she was so impressed with his inventions. Charles is famous for designing the world's first computer, the 'Difference Engine', which could perform calculations with numbers.

**" Religion to me is science, and science is religion. "**

Augusta Ada, Countess of Lovelace

**" The more I study, the more insatiable do I feel my genius for it to be. "**

He also had plans for an 'Analytical Engine' that would be able to handle even harder mathematical calculations. Because she was so good at languages as well as numbers, Ada was asked to translate an article about the machine, by an Italian mathematician called Luigi Menabrea, from French into English. But clever Ada added her own notes and ideas, too, and the article — which was called: 'Sketch of the Analytical Engine, with Notes from the Translator' — was published in a British science journal in 1843.

## SHAKING THE WORLD

Ada's groundbreaking idea was that codes could be created so that the 'Analytical Engine' could handle letters and symbols as well as numbers. She had another idea, too, about how the device might repeat a sequence of operations. This is called 'looping' and it is how computer programmes work today. Because of her detailed theories about how computers might work, many people consider her to be the world's first computer programmer. Charles Babbage may have designed the machine, but Ada had incredibly advanced ideas about how it might be used, not just for calculations, but for creative purposes, too, such as making music.

Sadly, Ada did not live to see her ideas become a reality. She died, poor and ill, at just 36 years old. It wasn't until nearly a hundred years later that her genius was recognised by mathematician and scientist Alan Turing as he worked on the first modern computers in the 1940s. She has been called 'the prophet of the computer age' because of her amazing vision about many of the things computers are able to do today.

# HYPATIA

## LIKE FATHER, LIKE DAUGHTER

Hypatia was born around the year AD 360 in Alexandria, Egypt. Founded by Alexander the Great around 332, Alexandria was an important ancient Greek city, a centre of learning and culture. It is best known for its important library and museum, where scholars met and studied its huge collection of around 700,000 scrolls.

It was here, during a time of many problems in Alexandria, that Hypatia grew up. The last professor at the University of Alexandria, her father, Theon, was a well-known mathematician, astronomer and writer, who passed all his knowledge on to his daughter. Hypatia spent much of her time at the library and museum, surrounded by her father's clever friends.

> **He who influences the thought of his times, influences all the times that follow. He has made his impression on eternity.**

## MATHS AND MURDER

Hypatia became the world's leading mathematician and astronomer, and the first known woman in these roles. She built on her father's ideas and wrote important works on geometry and numbers. She was a well-liked and highly respected teacher, showing her students how to design tools to study the stars, helping them to understand numbers, and sharing her knowledge of ancient philosophy.

> **Reserve your right to think, for even to think wrongly is better than not to think at all.**

She was a pagan, which meant that she did not follow Christianity. She gave hugely popular public lectures all over the city, telling people about the work of the ancient philosophers Plato and Aristotle. Hypatia was extremely well-liked by her audiences for her clear, logical speeches, her warmth and her love of knowledge. Her teaching and lectures — as well as her beauty — brought her many admirers, even though as a Neoplatonist she chose not to marry.

But as Hypatia's popularity grew, so did Alexandria's problems. Divisions between Christians, Jews and pagans had troubled Alexandria for many years — and those divisions were getting deeper. When Christianity became the main religion around the Mediterranean world, the Roman emperor Theodosius I decided to erase all traces of paganism. Under his rule, the archbishop Theophilus destroyed the great library at Alexandria in 391.

Hypatia invented two important things: the astrolabe (above) and the hydrometer

Hypatia of Alexandria

Hypatia soon found herself in great danger, accused of being a witch by Christian extremists who did not like her ideas. She had become a symbol of all they feared and misunderstood about the pagans. Then, one terrible day, a man called Peter the Lector led an angry mob in a terrible attack on Hypatia. They pulled her from her carriage, beat her to death and burned her body. Her shocking murder was a sign of the times: religious conflict had destroyed the priceless library and now it was responsible for the killing of a brilliant woman, the last great thinker of Alexandria.

**"** Life is an unfoldment and the further we travel the more truth we can comprehend. To understand the things that are at our door is the best preparation to understand the things that lie beyond. **"**

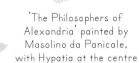

'The Philosophers of Alexandria' painted by Masolino da Panicale, with Hypatia at the centre

## SHAKING THE WORLD

Hypatia's brutal murder was a tragic reminder of the terrible things that can happen when people give in to hatred and fear. Her father had been the last known member of the great museum of Alexandria, and Hypatia was the last scholar in a time when science and scholarship were losing their value. She was a victim of religious extremism, and her death became a warning about what can occur when people stop listening to one another and stop respecting one another's beliefs. Her writing and teaching were important, showing the world for the first time that women could be great mathematicians, but her violent death also turned Hypatia into a powerful symbol of the importance of tolerance and understanding.

# ROSALIND FRANKLIN

## Chemist who discovered the structure of DNA

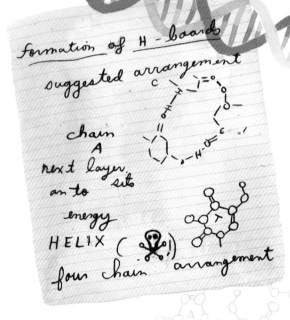

### INCREDIBLE INTELLIGENCE

Rosalind was born in the Notting Hill area of London in 1920, and grew up in a wealthy and well-educated Jewish family. She had four siblings and their father was a partner at a bank as well as owning a publishing company. The family loved foreign travel and hiking, which remained Rosalind's favourite activities for the rest of her life.

She was incredibly intelligent and was especially good at languages. She could have done any number of things, but she decided at a young age that she wanted to be a scientist when she grew up.

Rosalind went to Newnham College at Cambridge University, and earned her degree in chemistry. Working in Paris, France, she learned to use x-rays as a way of studying objects and what they are made of, and became a pioneer in this new technique, called x-ray crystallography.

*Rosalind Elsie Franklin*

### BRILLIANCE AND BETRAYAL

Working at King's College London, Rosalind and her student Raymond Gosling used x-ray crystallography to take pictures of DNA. DNA is short for 'deoxyribonucleic acid' and it contains instructions in codes that we call genes. Genes tell the cells in our bodies how to make a certain protein, and those proteins tell our cells how to grow and work. If a cell were like a computer, then the DNA would be the computer program that makes it work. Our DNA is made of chromosomes inherited from our parents and it makes us who we are.

> **66** All that is necessary for faith is the belief that by doing our best we shall come nearer to success and that success in our aims ... is worth attaining. **99**

Rosalind's x-ray diffraction photograph of DNA, taken before Watson and Crick discovered DNA's structure

A Swiss biologist called Friedrich Miescher had first identified DNA in 1869, but scientists were still puzzling out how it worked. Under a microscope it looked like long, single strands, but then Rosalind and her student took a picture, called Photograph 51, showing that DNA had what is called a 'double helix'. This was a huge breakthrough: DNA was no longer a mystery, and could begin to be decoded.

**" Science and everyday life cannot, and should not be separated. "**

But Rosalind lived and worked in a time when women were often not considered as clever as men and were not always treated well by the men they worked with. Even though Rosalind was a brilliant scientist, she worked with men who were uncomfortable with her success. One of those scientists, Maurice Wilkins, did not get on well with Rosalind and — without her knowledge or permission — showed 'Photograph 51' to two men called James Watson and Francis Crick. They realised that it was a very important discovery and used her photograph, as well as some of her other observations, to create a double-helix model of DNA that is now very famous.

**" Science, for me, gives only a partial explanation for life. In so far as it goes, it is based on fact, experience and experiment. "**

Then Rosalind discovered she had cancer. She carried on working for another two years, but died very young, at the age of 37. Four years after her death, Watson, Crick and Wilkins won the Nobel Prize for discovering the chemical structure of DNA, not revealing that it was Rosalind's work and photograph that helped give them their idea. Rosalind did not live to see her discovery change how scientists understand the human body, or how it helped to make important advances in medicine.

A portrait of Rosalind taken in 1956

## SHAKING THE WORLD

Rosalind changed science forever with her discovery of the structure of DNA. She also studied RNA, or ribonucleic acid, which is a copy of DNA that the body makes in the next step of creating proteins. Although she wrote many papers and helped build an understanding of many diseases, including polio, she was not given proper credit for her huge discovery. She was a brilliant scientist who changed the world forever, by helping other scientists understand that DNA is the building block of all life, but it is only recently that the world has begun to realise just how important Rosalind was.

# MARY ANNING

## SHE SELLS SEASHELLS

Mary was born in Lyme Regis, on the south coast of England, in 1799. Her parents, Richard and Mary, were poor, even though Richard worked hard as a carpenter to feed his family of nine children. Little Mary was a bright, curious child. Some people say that when she was just a year old she survived a lightning strike, which killed three other grown-ups. At the time, everyone thought it made her cleverer, but we know now it just meant that she was very lucky!

Mary loved to walk along the seashore, looking for fossils and seashells, which she sold to tourists. She was in just the right place for her hobby, because the coast near her home is one of the most important locations for fossils of the Jurassic period. But at that

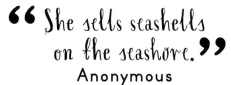

Mary, aged 12, discovering the first ichthyosaur found in England

time knowledge about dinosaurs and fossils was very limited. Fossils were called 'dragon's teeth' and were believed to be the stuff of myth and legend, not scientific fact. Geology was a brand-new science, and people did not trust it: the Bible's story of creation was the only accepted version of the history of the world, and the notion of evolution was only just coming into being.

When Mary was 11, her father died, and suddenly it became much more important to earn money selling the fossils she found, so that she could help feed her family. In fact, it is believed that the traditional tongue-twister: "She sells seashells on the seashore" was inspired by Mary.

Mary Anning

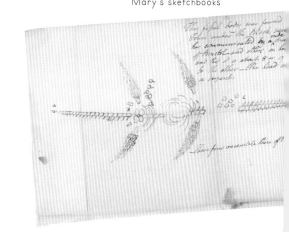

Pages from Mary's sketchbooks

> **" She sells seashells on the seashore. "**
> Anonymous

## DISCOVERING DINOSAURS

Mary began to spend all her time fossil-hunting, and not long after her father's death, she and her brother Joseph discovered a huge skeleton. As they worked to uncover it, they realised they had found the bones of a huge prehistoric sea creature: it was the first complete ichthyosaur ever discovered!

At the age of 12, Mary suddenly became one of the world's most famous palaeontologists, or scientists who study fossils. She was a very unlikely scientist: with no formal training and little education, living in poverty, she had to continue selling fossils just to help make ends meet for her family.

> **"[There is a] connection of analogy between the creatures of the former and present world."**

She and her trusty dog, Tray, scoured the seashore every day, searching tirelessly. Many of the fossils she found were the rather unglamorous sort: coprolites, or fossilised poo, in which Mary soon became a respected expert.

Several years later, Mary made her next great discovery. Her drawing of the plesiosaur that she found was so good, other scientists did not believe her at first. No one had ever seen one before and this new discovery earned Mary huge respect from her fellow palaeontologists. In 1828, she made another great find: the first pterosaur — or flying reptile — to be found in Great Britain, and the first complete skeleton found anywhere in the world. Although as a woman she could not be a full member, Mary was finally made an honorary member of the prestigious Geological Society in London, England.

> **"The carpenter's daughter has won a name for herself, and deserved to win it."**
> **Charles Dickens**

## SHAKING THE WORLD

Even though Mary was not properly credited in the museums where her finds were displayed, her discoveries shook the scientific world. She made some of the most important geological finds of all time. Mary's work, and her ideas about how the past and present were connected, paved the way for scientists such as Charles Darwin. Her discoveries helped Darwin and other scientists build their ideas about evolution, showing that the earth was much older than previously believed and that it had once been full of creatures who were now extinct.

We will never know what other discoveries Mary might have made because she died very young. But her short life was hugely important: her discoveries helped establish geology as a new and respected area of science, creating new ways of thinking about the history of the Earth and changing science forever.

# KATHERINE JOHNSON

Pioneering NASA mathematician and physicist

## MAGIC NUMBERS

Katherine Coleman was born in 1918 in a small town in West Virginia, in the USA, the youngest of four children. Her father, Joshua, worked as a farmer, lumberjack and handyman, while her mother, Joylette, was a teacher. Katherine couldn't wait to start school. She was brilliant with numbers and, by the time she was 10, she was in a class with 14-year-olds. This was especially impressive, because at that time, most African Americans had to stop school aged only 13.

Katherine's father wanted his clever daughter to have a better future. He moved the family so she could go to the very best schools. She finished high school at 14, and graduated with highest honours from her university at 18, before she began work as a teacher. She wanted to keep learning, though, and during a time when most American schools and universities were segregated (teaching only white or black people) she was chosen to become one of the first three black students to be offered a place on West Virginia State University's postgraduate programme, where she specialised in maths.

Katherine whilst working at NASA

## HUMAN COMPUTER

But Katherine soon left to have a family and she and her husband, James Goble, had three little girls: Constance, Joylette and Katherine. When the girls were older, she found out about a programme at the National Advisory Committee for Aeronautics in Langley, Virginia, which later became NASA. She started working there in 1953 and her new boss, Dorothy Vaughan, immediately saw that Katherine was special.

*66 Maths — it's just there. You're either right or you're wrong. That's what I like about it. 99*

Katherine was chosen to calculate the trajectory — the path of a flying object — for Alan Shephard, the first American astronaut in space. She worked on the flight paths that took the *Apollo 11* crew to the Moon and safely back. She also helped to bring the stranded astronauts on *Apollo 13* back to Earth. Some of her calculations were so long and complex that she had to stand on a ladder, starting her equations at the top of a huge blackboard near the ceiling and working her way down to the floor.

*Katherine Coleman Goble Johnson*

> 66 I counted everything.
> I counted the steps to the road,
> the steps up to church, the number
> of dishes and silverware
> I washed ... anything that
> could be counted, I did. 99

After her husband died, Katherine cared for her three girls on her own, while working as a full-time human computer for NASA. A few years later, she met and married James Johnson, who supported his wife in her amazing work. Soon, her reputation was so strong that the astronaut John Glenn requested that she double-check all the computer-calculated trajectories for his Friendship 7 mission in 1962, where he would be launched into space to orbit the Earth. Katherine remembers him saying: "If she says they're good, then I'm ready to go."

> 66 Everything is
> physics and maths. 99

Katherine using a computer at NASA Langley Research Center in 1980

## SHAKING THE WORLD

As one NASA official said, Katherine "literally wrote the textbook on rocket science". She did the calculations for many other important space missions, working for NASA for nearly 30 years until her retirement in 1986. When she was 97, she was awarded the Presidential Medal of Freedom, the highest honour in the USA, by President Obama.

Katherine's many achievements are especially extraordinary because, at the time of her most pioneering work, the American South was still divided by race. Katherine continues to encourage young people — including her 11 great-grandchildren — to study technology, science, engineering and maths. She keeps her eyes on the stars ... and her feet firmly on the ground.

# DOROTHY HODGKIN

Pioneering chemist and Nobel Prize winner

## CRYSTALS AND CHEMISTRY

Dorothy as a young woman

Dorothy Mary Crowfoot was born in 1910 in Egypt, to English parents called Grace and John, both of whom were archaeologists. Dorothy and her three younger sisters were sent back to England for school, joining their parents on digs during their holidays. When she was 10, Dorothy became interested in crystals, and her mother encouraged her passion, giving her books about chemistry. Dorothy liked archaeology, too, especially drawing ancient mosaics . . . but she loved chemistry even more.

At secondary school, Dorothy fought hard to be allowed to study science with the boys. At Somerville College, Oxford, in England, she became only the third woman ever to earn a high-class honours degree in chemistry at Oxford.

## DISCOVERIES AND DETERMINATION

Dorothy's fascination with crystals soon led her to unlock many scientific mysteries. Organic compounds are made up mainly of carbon, as well as other elements, and they are the building blocks of all life. Dorothy was one of the first scientists to use a method called 'x-ray crystallography' — where scientists take pictures of tiny crystals — to study organic compounds. Dorothy had a special gift for working out how nature builds these compounds, which would lead to many important discoveries.

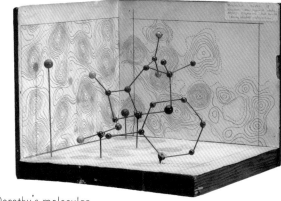

Dorothy's molecular model of penicillin

Dorothy continued working at Oxford, while raising her three children, even though she had painful rheumatoid arthritis, an illness that crippled her hands and fingers, making her work even more challenging. But Dorothy was determined. At first, she worked mainly on the study of insulin, which helps control the amount of sugar in blood. But, in 1939, she was asked to stop and try to work out the structure of penicillin instead. The structure of a molecule is a bit like a 3D puzzle; scientists need to figure out how a molecule is put together in order to understand how it works. Discovered in 1928 by Alexander Fleming, penicillin is a medicine used to stop bacterial infections, but it was hard to make it in large amounts. When Dorothy discovered how it was put together in nature, it became possible to make penicillin in laboratories in large enough quantities to help millions of people.

**" I was captured for life by chemistry and by crystals. "**

**" The detailed geometry of the coenzyme molecule as a whole is fascinating in its complexity. "**

Dorothy then started working on vitamin B12, which helps make DNA and red blood cells. If people don't have enough of it, they can become very ill. She and her team discovered that it was more complex than any organic compound studied before. She used computers to carry out difficult calculations, one of the first times this had been done.

Dorothy's discovery showed not just how vitamin B12 worked, but also how different kinds of chemistry were linked in ways not previously understood.

Dorothy Mary Crowfoot Hodgkin

In 1964, Dorothy was awarded the Nobel Prize for chemistry for her work on penicillin and vitamin B12, and she is still the only British woman to have won a Nobel Prize in science. Then, determined to understand the puzzling truth about insulin, Dorothy returned to her earliest studies. Finally — 34 years after she first worked on it — her persistence paid off: she discovered the structure of insulin. It was so complex that she'd had to wait until computers became advanced enough to help her with her work.

**"I seem to have spent much more of my life not solving structures than solving them."**

Dorothy with one of her models of a protein structure

## SHAKING THE WORLD

Not only did Dorothy lead the way as a chemist when very few women were encouraged to study science, she also made major discoveries about some of the most important and complex substances in the human body and in medicine. She helped other scientists understand how atoms and molecules work. Dorothy was not only extremely clever and hard-working, but also gentle, modest and well-liked by everyone who worked with her.

Lecturing all over the world about insulin and its importance in treating illnesses such as diabetes, Dorothy also fought to improve education, both in Britain and in developing countries, and worked with scientists from many different nations to find peaceful ways to make the world a better place. She was a gifted chemist who made groundbreaking discoveries — and a firm believer in the power of science to do good.

# DIAN FOSSEY

**Scientist who changed how we see gorillas**

Dian Fossey

### ANIMAL LOVER

Dian was born in San Francisco, California, USA, in 1932. She loved animals from a young age, and started horse-riding lessons when she was six. She became an excellent rider and an even better student. At university, she started studying business, but then decided to become a pre-veterinary student, before eventually training as an occupational therapist. She worked at a children's hospital, but her love of animals continued as she lived on a farm, helping to care for the animals there.

Dian in London, England, one year before her death

Dian longed to travel to Africa, so she carefully saved her money for a trip around the continent. Excited and intrigued, she travelled up into the mountains of Uganda, where she got her first glimpse of wild gorillas. Her life was changed forever.

### GORILLAS IN THE MIST

Back in the USA, Dian worked hard for many years, planning and earning money to return to Africa. Then she got a job leading a study on mountain gorillas, first in Zaire and later in Rwanda. Quietly, respectfully and patiently, she waited and watched. She began to understand the gorillas, and copied their behaviours — like walking on her knuckles and chewing on celery — so they would trust her. Dian befriended several groups of gorillas, using their individual 'noseprints' to tell them apart. She spent years watching them and making careful notes.

Because of films like *King Kong*, people wrongly believed that gorillas were vicious, but Dian was determined to make the world see how gentle these beautiful animals were. In the thousands of hours she spent watching them, she saw less than five minutes of aggressive behaviour — none of it towards humans. Although she knew a lot about gorillas already, she wanted to learn more and so she completed a PhD in animal behaviour at Cambridge University in England, earning greater respect and more money for her research.

**❝I feel more comfortable with gorillas than people.❞**

Dian playing with a baby gorilla

> **"** The more you learn about the dignity of the gorilla, the more you want to avoid people. **"**

But the gorillas were in great danger: their population had dropped to just 254 in the mid-1980s. Dian was desperate to learn all she could about them and even more desperate to stop them from vanishing altogether. She worried about the dangers gorillas faced from poachers — people who hunted illegally in national parks — because although gorillas weren't usually the real targets, they often got tangled in traps set for other animals. She believed in 'active conservation', forming anti-poaching patrols, wearing masks to scare off poachers, and spray-painting cattle to stop herders bringing them into the national park and damaging the gorillas' habitat. These actions made her unpopular with the locals, but she carried on.

> **"** The man who kills the animals today is the man who kills the people who get in his way tomorrow. **"**

Dian cared for all the gorillas she studied, but her favourite was Digit, who became her very close friend. Then tragedy struck: Digit was brutally killed by poachers as he tried to defend his family. Dian was heartbroken, furious and determined to do something. She wrote a book, called *Gorillas in the Mist*, which was later made into a film, to raise awareness of the plight of the gorillas. Then, just like Digit before her, her own life was cut terribly short: in her hut in Rwanda, Dian was murdered. No one knows exactly who killed her, or why. She was buried next to her beloved Digit.

## SHAKING THE WORLD

Dian's work with the mountain gorillas of Africa changed the way the world saw these amazing creatures. Her work has led to great conservation efforts and, although their future remains uncertain, the mountain gorilla population is now slowly increasing. Sadly, Dian did not live to see how her work has helped to rescue them from the brink of extinction but, by 2012, there were believed to be 880 gorillas in the wild — nearly four times the number left when she was still alive — with 24 new babies born in 2015. This is almost entirely due to the efforts of Dian, the gorillas' greatest protector and friend.

# VALENTINA TERESHKOVA

First woman to travel in space

## PASSION FOR PARACHUTES

Valentina Vladimirovna 'Valya' Tereshkova was born in 1937 in a village in western Russia. Her father, Vladimir, was a tractor driver, but was killed in the Second World War when little Valentina was just two years old. Her mother, Elena, raised Valentina, her sister Ludmilla and her brother Vladimir, working in a textile mill to earn money. Valentina started school when she was around eight and, when she was 17, she joined her mother working in the mill.

Valentina on a 1963 stamp from the Soviet Union

Valentina as a young woman on the airfield of the Yaroslav Flying Club

Valentina was very clever and, although she had to work to help earn money, she carried on with her studies at home. She also learned how to parachute for fun. She loved it, jumping whenever she could, day and night, on land and on water — but she didn't tell her mother! A few years later, her passion for parachuting got her an amazing job: she was chosen to train as a cosmonaut in the Soviet Union's space programme.

## SHOOTING FOR THE STARS

The Soviet Union (or USSR) and the United States were locked in a fiercely competitive 'Space Race', from the end of the 1950s through the 1960s. Although the USA and the USSR had been allies in the Second World War, the former friends stopped trusting each other. Soon, the world's two big 'superpowers' were stuck in a Cold War: there was no actual fighting, but both nations lived in constant fear of nuclear war. Space became the new frontier where the two nations could compete, each fighting to prove that they had better technology and therefore more power.

**" Hey, sky, take off your hat. I'm on my way! "**

Valentina Vladimirovna Tereshkova

The Soviets launched the first satellite, Sputnik, into space in October 1957. A month later, inside Sputnik II, Laika the space dog proved that it was possible to travel in space with the right equipment. In 1959, the Soviet space probe Luna 2 landed on the Moon; in 1961, Yuri Gagarin became the first astronaut — or cosmonaut as he was called in Russia — to go into space. The Soviets were clearly winning the Space Race!

Keen to keep their lead by sending the first woman into space, they trained four female cosmonauts. Valentina was the only one chosen for space flight. On 16 June 1963, she climbed aboard *Vostok 6* and took off, orbiting Earth an impressive 48 times in just under three days. Yuri Gagarin had orbited only once and the four American astronauts who followed him orbited a total of 36 times, so Valentina's success made her country very proud.

> **"** A bird cannot fly with one wing only. Human space flight cannot develop any further without the active participation of women. **"**

But she very nearly did not come back. Although the USSR kept it secret for decades, Valentina recently revealed how she realised that the calculations for her re-entry to the Earth's atmosphere were wrong: she knew that she would be sent hurtling out into space, never to return, unless she changed the coordinates. With the correction safely made, Valentina returned, making her greatest parachute jump yet: leaving her spacecraft, she fell 20,000 feet (over 6,000 metres) back to Earth.

## SHAKING THE WORLD

Valentina was called a 'Hero of the Soviet Union', the highest honour in the USSR. The Soviets continued to lead the Space Race, sending up the first three-man flight and achieving the first spacewalk. Then the USA finally pulled from behind to land men on the Moon, in what many believe was the greatest moment of the Space Race. But the first American female astronaut, Sally Ride, did not go into space until 20 years after Valentina made her voyage.

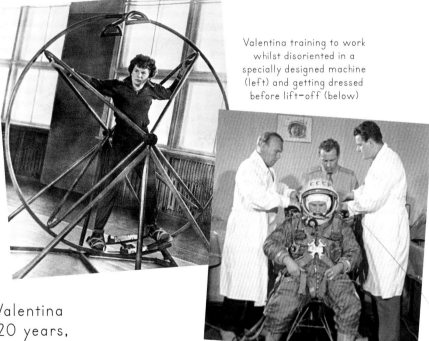

Valentina training to work whilst disoriented in a specially designed machine (left) and getting dressed before lift-off (below)

An important member of the Communist Party, Valentina led the Soviet Committee for Women for nearly 20 years, often representing her country abroad. When *Vostov 6* was displayed in London, England, in 2015, Valentina came to the opening ceremony and called her spacecraft, "my best and most beautiful friend". She and her trusty friend had indeed been on an incredible journey to the stars — and back again.

> **"** Once you've been in space, you appreciate how small and fragile the Earth is. **"**

85

# MALALA YOUSAFZAI

## Champion for education for women and girls

### EDUCATION FOR EVERYONE

Malala was born in a shack in the mountainous Swat Valley of northern Pakistan in 1997. Her father, Ziauddin, and her mother, Tor Pekai, named their daughter after a female Afghan hero who led a battle against the British. Little did they know that their own Malala would grow up to be a warrior, too.

Malala's family are from the Yousafzai tribe of the Pashtun people, who live in northern Pakistan and in Afghanistan. Like nearly all Pashtuns, they are Muslim and believe deeply in the teachings of the Qur'an. Tor Pekai left school at the age of six, when she realised that she would never get a job and would be expected to stay at home. But Ziauddin became a teacher and started a school, called Khushal School, because he believed that everyone has the right to education, no matter who they are.

> ## " If people were silent, nothing would change. "

In northern Pakistan, many marriages are arranged, but Tor Pekai and Ziauddin married for love and were very happy. Like her younger brothers, Khushal and Atal, Malala enjoyed her studies at school . . . until things started to change.

Malala Yousafzai

### TALIBAN TERROR

The Taliban is a group of extreme Pashtuns, who fought their way to power in Afghanistan, just over the border from where Malala and her family lived. Their rules meant that girls could not go to school and women were allowed to leave the house only with their father, husband or brother.

Malala (right) with her parents and younger brothers

After a terrible earthquake, things became even more difficult when the local Taliban leader told people they had to stop dancing, playing games, watching TV and listening to music. They forbade girls from going to school. Malala kept going to school in secret for as long as she could, wearing ordinary clothes instead of her uniform and hiding her books.

> ## " One child, one teacher, one book, one pen can change the world. "

Malala's father disagreed with the Taliban and spoke out against them on the radio. Malala joined her father, speaking to journalists and helping to make a documentary about her experience as a girl living under Taliban rule. She started a blog writing as 'Gul Makai', a female Pashtun hero who tried to teach people that fighting was wrong. Although the Taliban often beat and even killed people who did not obey them, Malala and her family continued to fight against the Taliban's rules, and her mother decided to start reading lessons.

In 2011, Malala received Pakistan's first National Youth Peace Prize and was nominated for the International Children's Peace Prize. This made the Taliban so angry that they decided to kill her. On 9 October 2012, as she rode home from school on the bus, two masked Taliban gunmen shot her in the head. The bullet went through her neck and shoulder, and two of her friends were injured as well. Malala survived, but she was so badly injured that she was flown to Birmingham in the UK for treatment. Her family joined her soon after. After many operations to repair her hearing and the nerves in her face, she finally left hospital in January 2013.

## SHAKING THE WORLD

Malala at the Nobel Peace Prize concert in Oslo, Norway

The whole world was united in their anger at the Taliban for trying to kill a schoolgirl. A petition with over two million signatures encouraged the government of Pakistan to create a new law, allowing all girls education. It was too dangerous for Malala and her family to return home, so the Pakistani government gave Ziauddin a job in education at the embassy and the family stayed in Birmingham. Malala began school in England, and did so well that she earned a place to study at Oxford University.

Malala continues to campaign for the rights of women and girls everywhere, meeting powerful leaders and speaking all around the world. She has received many honours and awards, including the Nobel Peace Prize in 2014. The youngest person ever to have received the award, she donated all the prize money to start a new secondary school for girls in Pakistan. A warrior of words, Malala has shown how one girl really can change the world.

*They are our most powerful weapons.* "

" *Let us pick up our books and our pens.*

# RIGOBERTA MENCHÚ

## MISTREATED MAYAS

Rigoberta Menchú was born in 1959 into a poor Mayan family in Guatemala. The next year, a violent civil war started to tear Guatemala apart, lasting for 36 years. During the war, the government changed many times, but its victims were always the same: the Mayas.

Rigoberta in front of the Pyramid of the Sun in Teotihuacan, Mexico

The Mayan people are indigenous to Guatemala, which means they have always been there, unlike the Latino Guatemalan people whose ancestors are Spanish. The Mayas — around half the population of Guatemala — have been treated brutally.

Their land has been taken from them to open silver mines, build farms and cut logs from the rainforests. Many Mayan people are still refused health care and jobs because they are a different race, but in Rigoberta's childhood, things were much worse.

Rigoberta Menchú Tum

> **66 This world's not going to change unless we're willing to change ourselves. 99**

Picking coffee beans in the mountains where they lived, Rigoberta's family often travelled to work on the coast, earning just a few pence a day. Farmers sprayed people and crops alike with dangerous pesticides, and workers were treated almost like slaves.

When she was a teenager, Rigoberta wanted to help change the lives of her people, especially women. Then her father, Vicente, was arrested by the army and hurt very badly. When he was freed, he worked to make things better for the Maya, and Rigoberta helped him.

## TERRIBLE TROUBLES

In 1979, Rigoberta's younger teenage brother was arrested and killed by the army. The next year, her father was killed in a fire while protesting peacefully. Then her mother was arrested and beaten so badly that she died, and another brother was killed by the army, too.

Rigoberta was heartbroken — but she wanted to fight back. She learned to speak Spanish as well as other Mayan languages, joined a strike to plead for better working conditions for farm workers, and marched in demonstrations. She also started educating her fellow Mayan people about how to resist the government and the army.

Around that time, the new government of General Montt and his army began a terrible project called 'Operation Sofia', destroying hundreds of indigenous Mayan villages. The army eventually 'disappeared' over 200,000 people, nearly all Mayas, pushing over 1.5 million people out of their homes and lands. Many — including Rigoberta — escaped to Mexico, but many others did not. The 'disappeared' people were kidnapped, killed and buried in unmarked graves. Mayan villages and crops were burned to the ground, making it impossible for them to return.

> **We are people and we want to be respected, not to be victims of intolerance and racism.**

Rigoberta continued to fight for indigenous people's rights from Mexico, helping to start 'The United Representation of the Guatemalan Opposition'. She shared her story with a writer called Elisabeth Burgos−Debray, and their book — *I, Rigoberta Menchú* — brought the world's attention to the terrible troubles in Guatemala. Rigoberta also narrated a film called *When the Mountains Tremble* about the awful ways her people have suffered.

## SHAKING THE WORLD

In 1992, Rigoberta was awarded the Nobel Peace Prize, in honour of her incredible work to improve the lives of the Mayan people. On the 500th anniversary of the year Columbus arrived in the Americas, Rigoberta was nominated by other indigenous people as a reminder of how many indigenous tribes were enslaved and killed, their land stolen and their cultures wiped out when Europeans arrived. She used the prize money to start the Rigoberta Menchú Tum Foundation.

Largely because of Rigoberta's work, and aided by Norway, a peace agreement was reached in 1996. Rigoberta created the first−ever indigenous political movement in Guatemala, called '*Winaq*', which means the 'Wholeness of the Human Being' in Mayan. She ran for president of Guatemala twice, becoming the first woman or Maya ever to run for leadership and, in 2011, Winaq won two seats in Congress. Since 1996, Rigoberta has been a UNESCO Ambassador for all the indigenous peoples of the world, working tirelessly to make sure they are treated equally and fairly.

> **During my most difficult moments and complex situations I have been able to dream of a more beautiful future.**

# AMELIA EARHART

Record-breaking pilot and adventurer

*Adventure is worthwhile in itself.*

## TOUGH TIMES

Born in 1897, Amelia Mary Earhart had a difficult childhood. Her mother did her best to raise Amelia and her sister Muriel, but her father, Edwin, was unwell and drank a lot. They were often poor and the girls spent a lot of time with their grandparents. Amelia became very independent. She liked to climb trees, hunt and play sports.

The first time Amelia saw an aeroplane at a state fair when she was 10 years old, she thought it was disappointing: "It was a thing of rusty wire and wood and not at all interesting," she said.

*Amelia as a young girl*

## TAKING FLIGHT

But once Amelia grew up, she changed her mind. One day at an air show, the pilot of a little red plane swooped towards her. Amelia was thrilled and felt as if the plane itself was telling her that she needed to fly. Not long afterwards, she flew for the first time and fell completely in love with flying.

Although she had trained as a nurse during the First World War, and later worked as a social worker, in her heart all Amelia really wanted to do was fly. She saved hard for lessons, cut her hair short, and even slept in her new leather pilot's jacket to make it look more worn, so that the other pilots wouldn't see how inexperienced she was. After six months, Amelia was able to buy a little yellow plane she called 'The Canary'.

A few years later, on 17 June 1928, she joined a team of male pilots flying from the USA across the Atlantic Ocean. They landed in Wales around 21 hours later, making Ameila the first woman to travel across the Atlantic by plane. Aeroplanes were a new invention, and they weren't safe: they were slow and loud and dangerous. Earlier that same year, three women had died trying to make the same crossing. Amelia's success made her a hero. Soon after, she married George Putnam, a book publisher who supported her love of flying.

*Amelia after crossing the Atlanic ocean*

Amelia and her husband made secret plans for her to become the first woman to fly solo across the Atlantic. Only one man, Charles Lindbergh, had done it before her. Flying solo was very hard: there were no computers in planes then, so usually you needed a navigator to guide you, a mechanic to fix things that went wrong, and a co-pilot so you could take breaks to eat and sleep. But on 20 May 1932, despite wind, ice and problems with the plane, Amelia did it — all on her own!

She set many other records, and was determined to take on the biggest challenge of all: becoming the first woman to fly around the world. On 1 June 1937, Amelia and her navigator set off. Over a month later, on 2 July, they had travelled all but the last 7,000 miles. They were aiming to stop on Howland Island, which is just 1.5 miles long, but after sending radio messages saying they were running low on fuel, the plane disappeared.

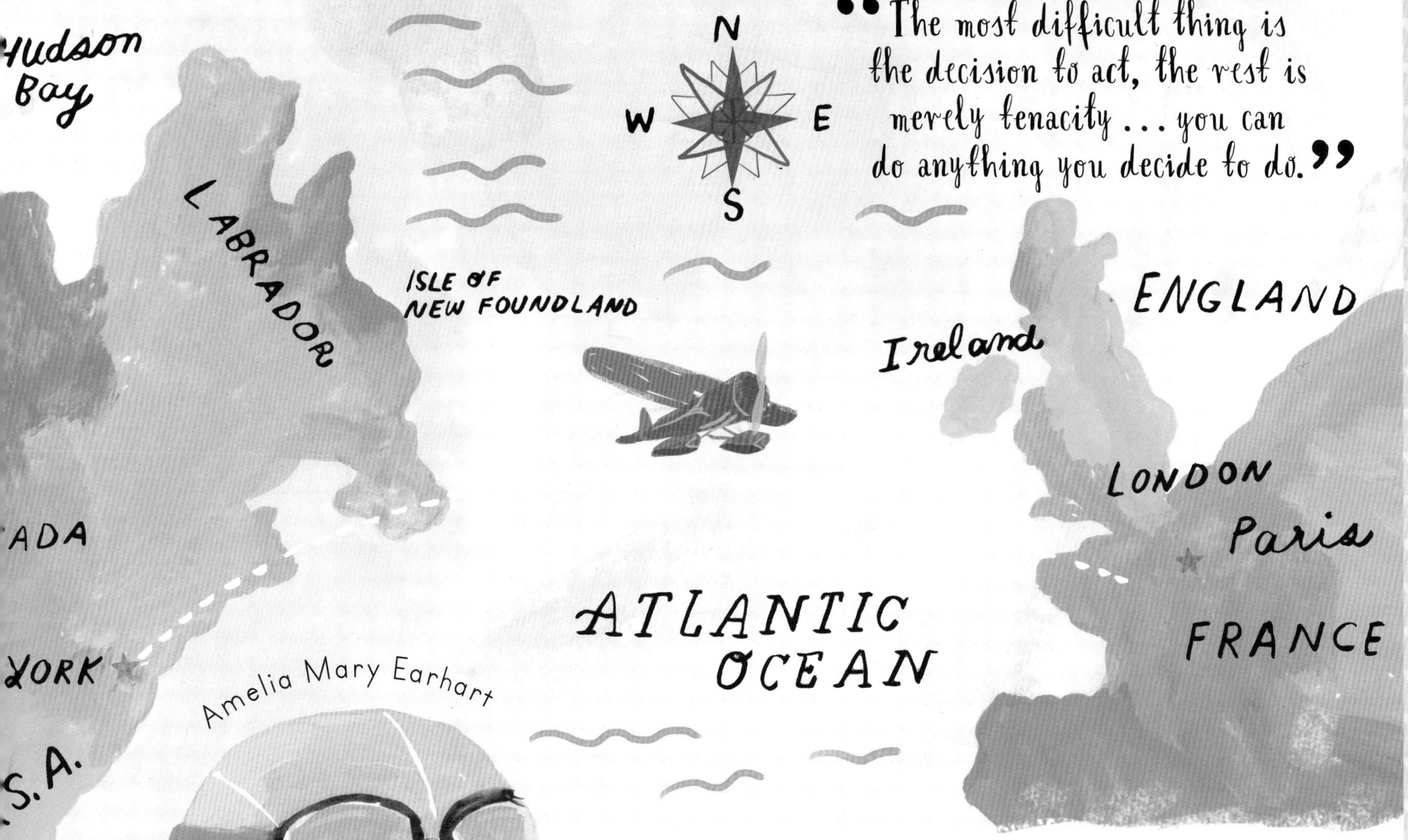
Hudson Bay
N
W
E
S
LABRADOR
ISLE OF NEW FOUNDLAND
ENGLAND
Ireland
LONDON
Paris
ADA
ATLANTIC OCEAN
FRANCE
YORK
S.A.

"The most difficult thing is the decision to act, the rest is merely tenacity ... you can do anything you decide to do."

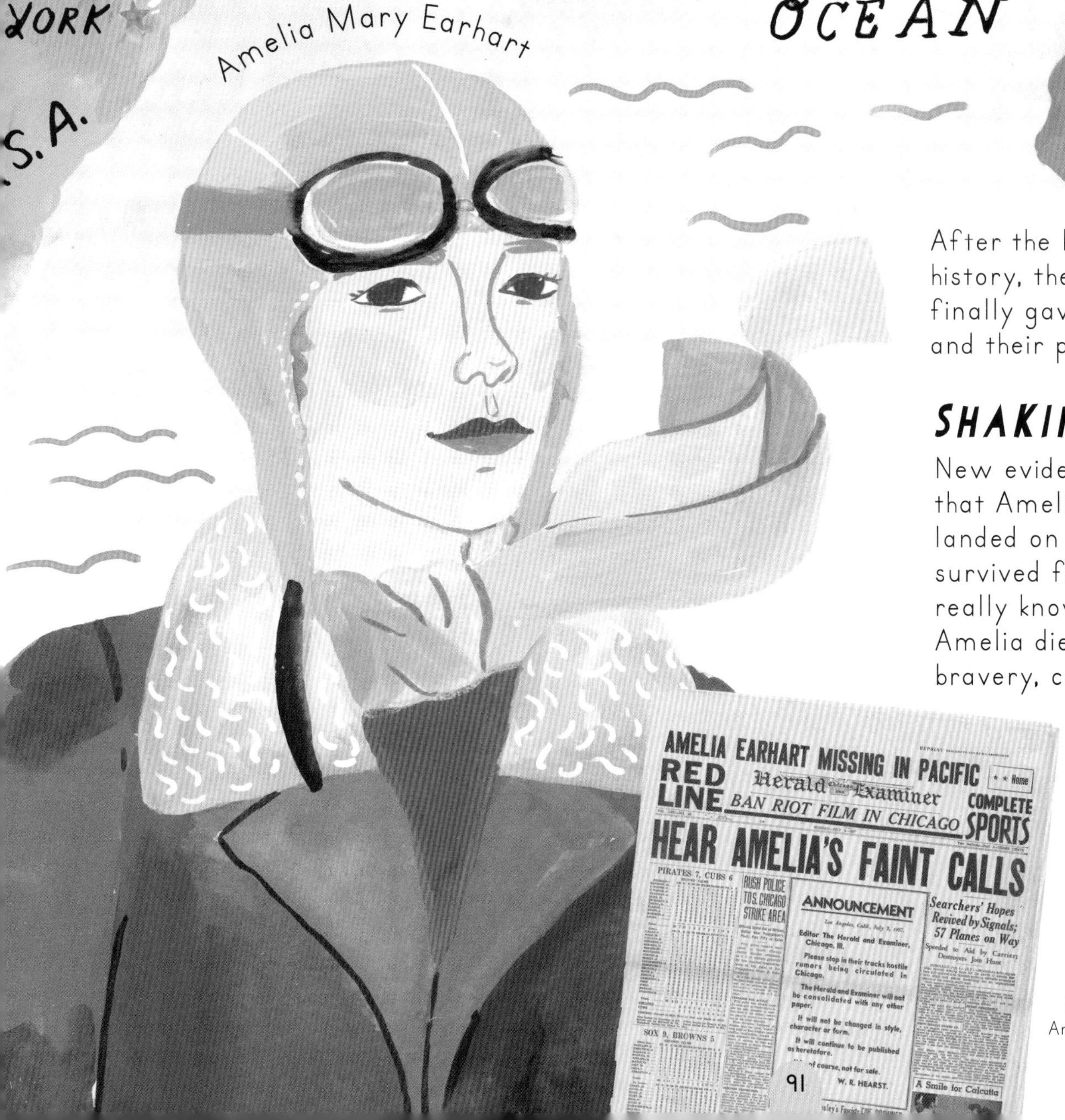
Amelia Mary Earhart
AMELIA EARHART MISSING IN PACIFIC
RED LINE
Herald Examiner
BAN RIOT FILM IN CHICAGO
COMPLETE SPORTS
HEAR AMELIA'S FAINT CALLS
ANNOUNCEMENT
Searchers' Hopes Revived by Signals; 57 Planes on Way

After the biggest air and sea search in history, the United States government finally gave up. Amelia, her navigator and their plane had simply vanished.

## SHAKING THE WORLD

New evidence has been found that shows that Amelia and her navigator may have landed on another uninhabited island and survived for a short time, but no one really knows what happened. Although Amelia died following her dream, her bravery, courage and strength live on.

"I am quite aware of the hazards. I want to do it because I want to do it."

Newspaper headlines after Amelia disappeared

# HANNAH SZENES

Jewish poet and Second World War hero

## HOPE FOR A HOMELAND

Hannah Szenes (pronounced 'Senesh') was born in Budapest, Hungary, in 1921. Her father, Béla, a well-known playwright and journalist, died when Hannah was six years old. Hannah's mother, Katherine, sent her to a Protestant private school, where Jewish families had to pay three times as much as Protestant and Catholic families. But because Hannah was so clever, her mother had to pay only twice as much. Hannah knew this was still very unfair and she did not like the way Jewish people were treated.

All over Europe during the 1920s and 1930s, Jewish people were being treated increasingly badly because of their religion and, although in Budapest they had greater freedom, Hannah dreamed of a fairer world. A movement called Zionism was growing stronger, as Jewish people like Hannah hoped for a Jewish homeland where they could live freely and happily. They called this idea of a homeland 'Eretz Israel'.

*Hannah Szenes*

> **" There is but one place on Earth in which we are not refugees, not emigrants, but where we are returning home: Eretz Israel. "**

Hannah joined a Zionist group for students, called Maccabea. When she graduated from school, she decided to leave behind her mother and her brother, György, and move to Palestine, where many Jewish people had gone to try and build a new homeland. She studied at an agricultural school for girls and joined a *kibbutz*, which was a type of farm where Jewish people lived and worked together. While she was there, Hannah wrote many poems, plays and songs. The most famous of these is called 'Eli, Eli (My God, My God)' and it is still sung today.

Hannah as a young woman

> **" I played a number in a game. The dice have rolled. I have lost. "**

## DANGEROUS MISSION

Hannah soon tired of tasks like doing laundry for nine hours every day, and longed to make a bigger impact. So Hannah joined the Haganah, which was a group of special fighters in Palestine that eventually became the Israel Defence Forces. Back in Europe, the Second World War had begun, and one of the main causes of the war was the terrible treatment of Jewish people by the German Nazi party and their leader Adolph Hitler. Hannah wanted to help fight the Nazis, so she joined the British Army in 1943, as part of the Women's Auxiliary Air Force, training to become a Special Operations Executive (SOE): Hannah was learning to be a spy.

After training in Egypt, Hannah parachuted into Europe, near the Hungarian border, working for three months with people who were fighting against the Nazis. But then, after she crossed into Hungary to help Jewish people there, things went badly wrong and Hannah was captured and arrested as a spy. For months, the police beat her very badly, even knocking out some of her teeth, but she refused to tell them anything about who she was or what she was doing. They then arrested her mother, threatening to kill her, but Hannah bravely refused to speak, saving her mother's life.

Women just like Hannah, training for the Women's Auxiliary Air Force

Despite being badly hurt, Hannah used a mirror to flash signals out of her window to the other prisoners and made letters that she held up to send messages, singing to keep the other prisoners from feeling sad and scared. The Nazis put Hannah on trial and, despite her bold speech warning that the war was near to an end and her captors would soon face judgement, too, Hannah was sentenced to death. Bravely refusing a blindfold so she could look her killers in the eye, she was murdered by a firing squad. Hannah was 23 years old.

## SHAKING THE WORLD

A national hero in Israel, Hannah dedicated her life to the dream of a Jewish homeland. Even though she lost her life fighting the Nazis, Hannah never lost hope. Writing in her diary every day, she sang and prayed to keep her spirits high. Her courage and vision made her a brave fighter for freedom, and her hope and belief lived on. Even though the Nazis killed her, they could never break her incredible spirit.

> **"A voice called, and I went. I went because it called."**

# ROSA PARKS

Leader in the campaign for racial equality in the USA

### DREAMS OF EQUALITY

Rosa Louise McCauley was born in 1913 in Tuskegee, Alabama, USA. When her parents separated, her mother, Leona, moved with Rosa and her younger brother, Sylvester, to her parents' farm. Rosa's grandparents, Rose and Sylvester Edwards, were former slaves. They taught her to believe that everyone was equal and that the colour of a person's skin didn't matter.

While the white children in town were driven to their brand-new school by bus, Rosa and her friends had to walk to their school, share one classroom and sit on the floor. But Rosa's mother believed that education was important and managed to send her daughter to a private secondary school. Rosa went on to train to be a teacher, but had to leave college to care first for her ill grandmother and then her mother.

### RIGHTS AND WRONGS

**" Knowing what must be done does away with fear. "**

Even though the US Civil War had ended nearly 50 years before Rosa was born, freeing all slaves, she was raised in a time when black people were treated very unfairly. African Americans were often hurt or even killed by some white people, especially in the southern United States.

*Rosa Louise McCauley Parks*

African Americans marching for equal rights in Washington, DC

Laws in the South kept black people separate, or segregated, from white people. There were laws saying that black people could not drink from the same water fountains, use the same toilets, go to the same schools, or sit in the same place on a bus as white people. Black people had to sit at the back of the bus, and bus drivers had the same power as police officers to enforce that rule.

After meeting her husband, Raymond Parks, and marrying him when she was 19, Rosa finally got her high school diploma. The couple lived in Montgomery, Alabama. Raymond worked as a barber and Rosa as a seamstress at a department store. He encouraged her to become involved in the early civil rights movement, a group of people who fought peacefully to make things better and fairer for black people.

> " Racism is still with us. But it is up to us to prepare our children for what they have to meet, and, hopefully, we shall overcome. "

On 1 December 1955, after a hard day at work, Rosa got on the bus to go home and sat at the back, as usual. The bus soon filled with so many white passengers that some were standing in the aisle. The driver decided to make the black section smaller and the white section bigger so more white people could sit down. He asked four black passengers to move further back. Three of those passengers got up, but Rosa Parks did not. "Why don't you stand up?" asked the driver. "I don't think I should have to stand up," Rosa replied. The driver called the police and Rosa was arrested.

Rosa said later that she wasn't so much physically tired, as tired of giving in. Inspired by Rosa, thousands of people decided to stop using the city's bus system, as a peaceful way of fighting the unfair rules. The Montgomery Bus Boycott started on 5 December 1955, led by a young man named Dr Martin Luther King, Junior. The city lost a lot of money as buses sat empty. The homes of Dr King and other leaders were bombed, churches were burned and violence broke out across the city. The boycott lasted for 381 days.

Rosa on a bus the day public transport was desegregated in the city

> " I would like to be remembered as a person who wanted to be free ... so other people would be also free. "

## SHAKING THE WORLD

Rosa's simple act of protest sparked huge changes in the South. Inspired by Rosa, her lawyer, Fred Gray, succeeded in making the courts agree that racial segregation on public transport was illegal.

Rosa became known as 'the mother of the US civil rights movement'. She started an institute to teach young people about civil rights; wrote two books and received many awards, including the Presidential Medal of Freedom and the Congressional Gold Medal, the two highest awards in the USA. But despite her fame and influence, she was always modest, saying, "All I was doing was trying to get home from work."

95

# NOOR INAYAT KHAN

Second World War secret agent and hero

## A PRACTICAL PRINCESS

Noor-un-Nisa Inayat Khan was born in snowy Moscow, Russia, on the first day of 1914. Her mother, Ora Ray Baker, was a tiny American woman of Irish, English and Scottish descent, and her father, Hazrat Inayat Khan, was a famous Indian musician and teacher of the mystic religion of Sufism. In fact, little Noor was an Indian princess, a direct descendent of Tipu Sultan, who was the Muslim ruler of Mysore in the 1700s. 'The Tiger of Mysore' had fought bravely against the British, as had his son, but the family kept quiet about their royal heritage so as not to cause problems with the British, who still ruled India.

Dreamy and delicate, Noor was also kind and generous. When she was four, living in London, England, she learned that many Russian children were hungry, so she started collecting chocolates to send them. Soon, the family moved to Paris, France, where Noor learnt perfect French, though she, her sister and her two brothers felt they were Indian, learning both Hindi and Urdu.

When she grew up, Noor started writing stories for children, which were collected in a book called *Twenty Jataka Tales*. But as the Second World War began, she started thinking more practically. Because the Sufi religion teaches peaceful non-violence, she and her siblings felt torn: how could they stand quietly by and let the Nazis carry out their terrible acts, without fighting back? One brother joined the French Resistance; the other went back to England to join the armed services, and Noor, her mother and her sister travelled with him.

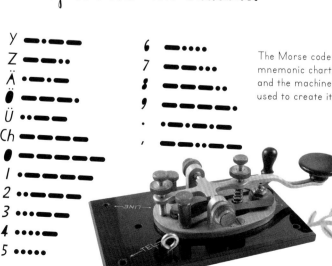

The Morse code mnemonic chart and the machine used to create it

> **"I wish some Indians would win high military distinction in this war. It would help to build a bridge between the English and the Indians."**

| | | | |
|---|---|---|---|
| A •— | M —— | Y —•—— | 6 —•••• |
| B —••• | N —• | Z ——•• | 7 ——••• |
| C —•—• | O ——— | Ä •—•— | 8 ———•• |
| D —•• | P •——• | Ö ———• | 9 ————• |
| E • | Q ——•— | Ü ••—— | 0 ————— |
| F ••—• | R •—• | Ch ———— | , •—•—•— |
| G ——• | S ••• | | |
| H •••• | T — | 1 •———— | |
| I •• | U ••— | 2 ••——— | |
| J •——— | V •••— | 3 •••—— | |
| K —•— | W •—— | 4 ••••— | |
| L •—•• | X —••— | 5 ••••• | |

## SECRET AGENT

As many Parisians fled, the Germans bombed those leaving the city. Noor and her family were horrified, renewing their promise to fight against the Nazis. On arrival in England, Noor joined the Women's Auxiliary Air Force and started learning Morse Code. Military Intelligence was watching her, impressed that she was bilingual in French and English.

Noor in her military uniform

Although Noor believed that India deserved to be free from British rule, she soon became a secret agent for Winston Churchill's British government. Noor was trained by the Special Operations Executive, learning to shoot guns, throw grenades and handle explosives. In June 1943, she became the first woman radio operator for the Allies to be sent into France. On her farewell visit with her family, she shared the happy news that she was engaged to be married to a British officer. She said her goodbyes and boarded the train. Noor would never see them again.

In Paris, Noor's codename was Madeleine, and she worked with the 'Prosper' radio team, spying on the Nazis and sending information by radio to the British government. Many members of the organisation were quickly arrested by the Germans, but she escaped, hiding all over France while she continued sending important information back to London. In October, though, she was betrayed by a Frenchwoman and arrested by the Gestapo, the Nazi secret police.

Noor briefly escaped but was recaptured and sent to Germany, where she was kept in chains in solitary confinement. The Nazis beat her repeatedly, but she refused to give them any information. She was kept prisoner for nearly a year and, during that whole time, Noor kept silent. In September 1944, she was moved to the concentration camp at Dachau, where she and three other female spies were shot and killed.

Noor-un-Nisa Inayat Khan

"Liberté" – Noor's final word before she was executed.

## SHAKING THE WORLD

Five years after her death, Noor was awarded the British George Cross and the French Croix de Guerre in recognition of her bravery and sacrifice. Like the other British spies she trained and worked with, Noor was deeply courageous. But unlike the others, she was fighting for a country that was not her own, a country against which her own family had fought for independence. She was a truly international person — Indian, American, British and French — who fought not for one country, but for a cause: to bring freedom to Europe.

A bust of Noor in Gordon Square Garden, London, England

NOOR INAYAT KHAN 1914-1944

# EMMELINE PANKHURST

Leader in the fight for women's votes

## EQUAL EDUCATION

Emmeline Goulden was born in 1858 in Manchester, England, the eldest of 10 children. Her family had a long tradition of being involved in politics and trying to change the world. Both her parents opposed slavery, fighting to help end it. They were also in favour of the new women's suffrage movement, which said that everyone should have the right to vote, including women.

Emmeline's mother took her to her first suffrage meeting when she was 14, yet Emmeline still felt that her parents treated her brothers' education as more important than her own. Luckily, the teachers at Emmeline's finishing school in Paris, France, believed that girls should not just learn embroidery but chemistry and bookkeeping too, so she returned to England with an education just as good as her five brothers had received.

A portrait of Emmeline

## SUFFERING FOR SUFFRAGE

When Emmeline grew up, she met a lawyer named Richard Pankhurst, who shared her belief that women deserved to be treated equally. In 1870 and 1882, Richard wrote the 'Married Women's Property Acts', which allowed married women to keep their property and money when they got married, instead of handing it all over to their husband as they'd had to do before.

Emmeline and Richard were soon married, and Emmeline was a busy wife and mother to their five children. But Emmeline did not just stay at home, as most women did at the time, and continued working on the suffrage movement. In 1889, she started the Women's Franchise League, which fought to allow married women to vote in local elections.

Suffragettes with placards in London, England

A few years later, Richard — who was 25 years older than Emmeline — suddenly died, leaving Emmeline shocked and broken-hearted. To pull herself out of her grief, she threw herself completely into her cause and, in 1903, Emmeline founded the Women's Social Political Union. Emmeline gave speeches all over the country, including to a crowd of half a million in Hyde Park in London.

66 We are here, not because we are law-breakers; we are here in our efforts to become law-makers. 99

66 Trust in God — she will provide. 99

Soon, tired of talking and getting nowhere, Emmeline and the other 'suffragettes' — including her daughters, Christabel and Sylvia — saw themselves as an army with a war to win. Adopting the motto 'Deeds not words', they became famous for doing whatever it took to make progress in the fight for women's votes. They smashed windows, started fires and went on hunger strikes. One of their members, Emily Davison, was killed when she threw herself under the king's horse in protest at the lack of change.

Emmeline being arrested outside Buckingham Palace, London, England

### Emmeline Pankhurst

In 1913, in response to the hunger strikes taking place all over the country, the government passed the so-called 'Cat and Mouse Act' that allowed hunger strikers to grow strong enough to be released . . . and then be arrested again. Emmeline herself was arrested many times and went on hunger strike in prison, which meant that the wardens force-fed her — a horrible and violent experience. But when the First World War broke out in 1914, Emmeline and her fellow suffragettes suddenly ended their protest activity, throwing all their energy into supporting the war effort instead.

> " . . . nothing on Earth and nothing in heaven will make women give way; it is impossible. "

### SHAKING THE WORLD

Because women worked hard in the war, both at home doing the jobs of men who were away at the front and as nurses on the battlefield, they finally began to be recognised as a crucial part of society. In 1918, their contribution was finally recognised in the 'Representation of the People Act', which allowed women over 30 the right to vote. Emmeline's hard work had finally paid off.

Then, in March 1928, a bill was introduced that would finally give all women true voting equality with men. The 'Equal Franchise Act' allowed women aged 21 or older the right to vote — just like men. Emmeline died just a few weeks before the act was passed into law, but she died knowing that the dream she had fought for would finally become a reality. As the fearless leader of the suffrage movement, Emmeline dedicated her life to earning equal rights for women — and she succeeded.

YES TO EQUAL RIGHTS FOR WOMEN!

# CATHY FREEMAN

## OVERCOMING OBSTACLES

Catherine Astrid Salome Freeman was born in Queensland, Australia, in 1973. Like many Aboriginal children, Cathy and her four siblings had a difficult life. After the arrival of the British in 1770, the Aboriginal people in Australia were treated terribly, killed by European diseases and murdered as the invading Europeans rushed to steal their tribal homelands.

Cathy as a young woman

These problems continued into modern times. Cathy's grandmother was part of the 'Stolen Generations'. For many years, Aboriginal children were taken from their homes and raised in state institutions, supposedly to protect them from poverty. Families were tragically broken apart and the stolen children were raised far from home, with little or no idea about who they really were. Luckily, this cruel policy ended just before Cathy was born, and she was raised by her own loving, attentive mother, who made sure that all her children were well fed, cared for and educated. Their father had many problems and left the family when Cathy was five.

Early on, her mother saw that Cathy had a special talent for running. When she was just eight, Cathy won her first race — even though she had a bandage over one eye — and became completely hooked on running. Cathy's stepfather also believed in her talent and became her first coach, encouraging Cathy to follow her dream of becoming an Olympic athlete.

"I definitely do things on my terms."

Catherine Astrid Salome Freeman

## VICTORY AND PRIDE

Everywhere Cathy went, she won. She worked hard — but it felt easy, because she loved to run. When she was 17, Cathy was named Young Australian of the Year; the next year, she became Aboriginal Athlete of the Year. Not long after that, in 1994, Cathy won her first gold medals at the Commonwealth Games.

She draped a flag around her shoulders for her victory lap . . . but the flag was not the Australian one. She proudly carried the Aboriginal flag: red for earth, yellow for sun and black for skin.

Shockingly, Cathy was criticised by the press for her action, and was warned not to do it again. But, when she won her next event, she bravely carried the Aboriginal flag once more. She knew who she was, and she wanted the whole world to know, too.

**"All that pain, it's very strong and generations have felt it."**

In 1996, Cathy achieved her childhood dream of becoming an Olympic athlete. She set four new Australian records and won a silver medal. Over the next few years, Cathy won an incredible 22 finals in a row, including two World Championships. A national hero, she was named Australian of the Year in 1998. But, although her running brought her fame and success, Cathy also suffered sadness: her sister Anne-Marie, who had cerebral palsy, died of an asthma attack and her father, Norman, died too.

They were not there to witness Cathy's proudest moment, but she dedicated her races to them. In 2000, at the Sydney Olympics, after lighting the Olympic flame, Cathy went on to win a gold medal in the 400-metres event with massive support from the crowds. This time, Cathy ran in red, yellow and black shoes and, when she won, she followed Aboriginal tradition, running her victory lap barefoot. She carried both the Australian and Aboriginal flags and, for the first time the press celebrated her choice. Australia's ideas about Aboriginal pride had changed — and Cathy had helped to change them.

**"Education is the key to a positive pathway."**

## SHAKING THE WORLD

Cathy retired from running at the age of 30. In 2007, she founded the Cathy Freeman Foundation, which encourages young Aboriginal people to stay in school. Remembering her own difficult school years, Cathy is committed to making life better for all young Australians.

She has faced many challenges in her life, but Cathy has worked hard to help young Aboriginals build positive self-esteem, which she lacked until she became a runner and running set her free. Cathy's incredible talent helped her to believe in herself and now she is sharing that belief with another generation, in the hope that they will feel pride in their Aboriginal heritage and be happy.

Cathy winning gold in the women's 400 metres final at the Sydney Olympics in Australia

# SOPHIE SCHOLL

## German anti-Nazi resistance leader

## FAMILY, FAIRNESS AND FREEDOM

Sophia Magdalena Scholl was born in 1921 in southwest Germany, to Robert and Magdalena Scholl, the fourth of six children. Sophie's father was the liberal mayor of the town and her mother raised her children to have a firm Christian faith and a strong conscience. Sophie loved to read and did brilliantly well in school.

Sophie as a young girl

But things began to change all over Germany as Hitler, leader of the Nazi party, rose to power. At home, Robert, was critical of the Nazis, but his children were curious about joining the massively popular Nazi youth groups. However, Sophie remained loyal to her Jewish friends, complaining when they were not allowed to join and reading aloud from a banned book by a Jewish author she admired.

In 1935, the Nuremberg Laws barred Sophie's Jewish friends from many normal activities and from attending Sophie's school. Then her older brother, Hans, was arrested by the Nazis for joining a more independent youth group, which affected Sophie deeply. Their father continued to encourage them to resist the Nazis, saying, "What I want for you is to live in uprightness and freedom of spirit, no matter how difficult that proves to be."

## THE ROSE OF RESISTANCE

Upset about the Nazis, Sophie started studying biology and philosophy at the University of Munich. Then Sophie's boyfriend, Fritz, fighting in the East, told Sophie about the terrible concentration camps. Sophie became even angrier when her father was arrested for criticising Hitler. Sophie's brother, Hans, and three friends then started an anti-Nazi group called the White Rose. Sophie joined immediately. Despite the dangers, they wanted to open the other students' eyes to the terrible crimes being committed by the Nazis.

**" Somebody, after all, had to make a start. "**

In 1942, copies of a leaflet called 'The White Rose' appeared around the university. In their essay about how the Nazi regime was destroying Germany, the authors called on people to rise up and resist. This was shocking and radical: it was the first time anyone in Germany had made such public criticism of the Nazis. Desperate to discover who was responsible, the Nazis could not find the culprits. Sophie, Hans and their friends made a second leaflet, then a third, a fourth and a fifth . . . Graffiti began to appear all over Munich: 'Down with Hitler!', 'Hitler the mass murderer!' and *'Freiheit!'* which means 'Freedom!'.

Bronze replicas of White Rose leaflets are scattered haphazardly across the pavement in Munich, Germany, as a memorial to the group

Then, on 18 February 1943, while passing out the newest leaflet, Sophie and Hans were spotted by a Nazi sympathiser. He called the German secret police, and Sophie, Hans and their friend Christoph were put on trial for treason. But their trial was just for show.

As the judge shrieked and roared, Sophie courageously announced, "What we wrote and said is also believed by many others. They just don't dare to express themselves as we did." But her bravery fell on deaf and angry ears, and all three were sentenced to immediate death. In her final visit with their parents, Sophie was calm and smiling. Just a few hours after the trial, first Sophie, then her brother and finally Christoph were executed by guillotine. Their brave resistance was over.

## SHAKING THE WORLD

The Irish statesman Edmund Burke once said, "The only thing necessary for the triumph of evil is for good men to do nothing." In the face of great evil, Sophie acted.

Sophia Magdalena Scholl

**"Stand up for what you believe in, even if you are standing alone."**

Believing that everyone deserved to be treated well, she was unable to sit by and watch as the Nazis committed so many horrific acts. Others, frightened and trying to keep themselves safe, perhaps shared her belief that the Nazis were wrong, but Sophie — along with Hans and the other members of the White Rose — refused to keep silent.

**"The sun still shines."**

The Nazis killed Sophie for speaking her mind, but they could not kill her spirit. Her life — and her death — are an incredible symbol of the power that one person can have, the change that one person can make, by standing up for what is right and good.

A marble bust of Sophie in the Walhalla memorial in Germany

# ANNE FRANK

**Second World War diary keeper**

## A GROWING DANGER

Anne as a young girl before the Second World War

Annelies Marie Frank was born in 1929 in Frankfurt am Main, Germany. Otto and Edith were loving parents to Anne and her older sister Margot. Anne was a real chatterbox who loved beach holidays and had many friends. The Franks were happy.

But danger loomed: Germany was becoming a frightening place. The new leader of Germany and the Nazi party, Adolf Hitler, planned to conquer all of Europe, but he also wanted to get rid of all Jewish people — like Anne and her family — as well as people with mental illnesses, Gypsies and many others. Hitler's programme, which eventually caused the deaths of over 11 million people, became known as the Holocaust.

Otto moved the family to Amsterdam in the Netherlands and for a while they felt safer. He started a new business and was a kind boss — a kindness that would later repay him well. But when the Nazis invaded the Netherlands, Jewish people started to disappear, with stories of terrible concentration camps in the East. Otto and Edith grew worried, and began to make plans.

## DIARY OF DREAMS

Anne's red checked diary, her first journal

On her 13th birthday, Anne was given a diary. She shared cookies at school and had a party with strawberry pie and a roomful of flowers. It was the last birthday Anne would celebrate in freedom.

Weeks later, the Nazis ordered Margot to report to a work camp . . . so the family went into hiding. Helped by Otto's loyal workers — especially Miep Gies — they moved into Otto's office, where a secret doorway disguised as a bookcase led to hidden rooms called 'the annexe'. Anne left behind her adored cat Moortje, her favourite bag of marbles, and all her many friends. No one knew where the Franks had gone: they simply vanished.

Anne (centre) with her father, Otto, and sister, Margot

> **" But where there's hope, there's life. It fills us with fresh courage and makes us strong again. "**

The Franks were joined by the Van Pels family and a dentist named Fritz Pfeffer. Behind the blackout curtains, they lived in complete secrecy, fearful that the tiniest bit of light or noise would give them away.

Annelies Marie Frank

> **"** I want to be useful or bring enjoyment to all people, even those I've never met. I want to go on living even after my death! **"**

Anne escaped the fear and hardship by writing in her red-and-white diary. Starting each entry "Dear Kitty", she wrote about her dreams: she wanted to live in Paris and London, to wear beautiful dresses and to become a journalist. She wrote about being hungry and bored. She wrote about her jealousy of Margot and arguments with her mother. She wrote about her feelings for 17-year-old Peter Van Pels and about their first kiss. She wrote about how she longed to play and run outside, instead of gazing out at a chestnut tree through a sliver of glass. But, most of all, she wrote about hope: hope that something would change and that she would be free once more.

After two years and 35 days, their hiding place was discovered, and the German secret police arrested them all. Anne, Margot and Edith were sent to the concentration camp at Auschwitz-Birkenau, where over a million people were killed — including Edith. After they were moved to the camp at Bergen-Belsen, the sisters got typhus. They died a few days apart — first Margot, then Anne. Anne was just 15 years old.

## SHAKING THE WORLD

Otto Frank was the only one of the eight to survive the horrors of the Holocaust. When he returned to Amsterdam, he found Miep. She had found Anne's diary and saved it but, respecting Anne's privacy, she had not read it. Otto decided to share Anne's story with the world and the diary was published in June 1947 — the year Anne would have turned 18. Now published in over 60 languages, her diary has been read by millions.

Anne's diary was given back to her father, Otto, after her death in a concentration camp

Anne never got to grow up, but her sense of humour, her imagination, her courage, her hopes and her dreams have been shared by people all over the world. Although her life was cut short, the beauty of Anne's spirit lives on.

> **"** ...I still believe, in spite of everything, that people are truly good at heart. **"**

# WHEN THEY WERE BORN

**Hatshepsut**
Around
1504 – 1458 BC

**Boudicca**
Around
AD 30 – 61

**Hypatia**
Around
AD 360 – 415

**Empress Wu Zetian**
AD 624 – 705

**Joan of Arc**
Around
1412 – 1431

**Isabella I**
1451 – 1504

**Mirabai**
Around
1498 – 1557

**Elizabeth I**
1533 – 1603

**Sacajawea**
1788 – 1812

**Mary Anning**
1799 – 1847

**Mary Seacole**
1805 – 1881

**Ada Lovelace**
1815 – 1852

**Emily Brontë**
1818 – 1848

**Florence Nightingale**
1820 – 1910

**Harriet Tubman**
Around
1820 – 1913

**Elizabeth Blackwell**
1821 – 1910

**Sarah Bernhardt**
1844 – 1923

**Emmeline Pankhurst**
1858 – 1928

**Annie Sullivan**
1866 – 1936

**Beatrix Potter**
1866 – 1943

**Marie Curie**
1867 – 1934

**Maria Montessori**
1870 – 1952

**Helen Keller**
1880 – 1968

Anna Pavlova
1881 — 1931

Coco Chanel
1883 — 1971

Georgia O'Keeffe
1887 — 1986

Amelia Earhart
1897 — 1937

Frida Kahlo
1907 — 1954

Rachel Carson
1907 — 1964

Dorothy Hodgkin
1910 — 1994

Mother Teresa
1910 — 1997

Rosa Parks
1913 — 2005

Noor Inayat Khan
1914 — 1944

Billie Holiday
1915 — 1959

Indira Gandhi
1917 — 1984

Katherine Johnson
1918

Eva Perón
1919 — 1952

Rosalind Franklin
1920 — 1958

Sophie Scholl
1921 — 1943

Hannah Szenes
1921 — 1944

Maya Angelou
1928 — 2014

Anne Frank
1929 — 1945

Dian Fossey
1932 — 1985

Valentina Tereshkova
1937

Wangari Maathai
1940 — 2011

Shirin Ebadi
1947

Theresa Kachindamoto
1958

Rigoberta Menchú
1959

Cathy Freeman
1973

Malala Yousafzai
1997

# GLOSSARY

**American Civil War** (1861–1865) The war fought in the United States, over the question of slavery, with the Union Army of the North (under the leadership of President Abraham Lincoln) eventually beating the Confederate Army of the South and freeing around four million slaves.

**Astronomy** The study of stars, planets, solar systems, galaxies and other objects beyond the Earth's atmosphere.

**Atom** The smallest particle of matter that can exist.

**Braille** A system of writing for blind people, made up of small raised bumps on the page that are interpreted through touch.

**Catholicism** The branch of the Christian church led by the Pope, with over one billion members.

**Chemistry** An area of science that deals with what substances are, how they are formed, and how they behave when changed.

**Cholera** A name for several different diseases that cause severe and sometimes life-threatening vomiting and diarrhoea.

**Chromosome** A part of the centre of a cell that contains most or all of the genes of a living being. Humans have 46 chromosomes, in 23 pairs.

**Civil rights** The benefits all citizens are owed as part of a society, especially to freedom, equality and fairness.

**Communist** A person or government who believes that everything should be shared and there should be no personal property.

**Concentration camp** A place where large numbers of prisoners are held and forced to work, without enough space, food or medical care, and are sometimes killed.

**Conservation** A special effort to protect and preserve something that is valuable, especially nature.

**Crimean War** (1853–1856) Fought between Russia and Great Britain, France and Turkey, mainly around the Black Sea and in what is now the Ukraine, over control of land as well as disagreements between the Russian Orthodox church, the Turkish Ottomans and the French Catholic church.

**Crystallography** The scientific study of how crystals are made, which aims to understand the structure of atoms and other materials.

**Democracy** A system of government where the people have the power to lead their own country, usually through freely elected leaders.

**DNA (deoxyribonucleic acid)** The material in nearly every living being that is inherited and the order of which decides our genetic makeup, working alongside its chemical cousin RNA (ribonucleic acid).

**Double helix** The spiral-ladder shape of DNA, made up of pairs of adenine, guanine, cytosine and thymine, which attach to sugar and phosphorus. Its pattern allows DNA to copy itself.

**Dynasty** A line of rulers from the same family.

**Element** A substance that is made entirely of one atom, which cannot be broken down into smaller parts and which is the base of all matter.

**Extremist** A person with very strong political or religious beliefs, who often takes part in violence or other illegal actions.

**Feminist** A person who believes that men and women are equal, and supports women's rights.

**First World War** (1914–1918) The war fought between the Central Powers (led by Germany) and the Allied Powers (led by Great Britain, France, Russia and the United States), over control of Europe, with the Allied Powers winning. Over 16 million people died.

**Fossil** The remains of a prehistoric plant or animal preserved in rock.

**Franco-Prussian War** (1870–1871) Also known as the Franco-German War, a group of German states, led by Prussia under Otto Von Bismarck, defeated France, ending France's position of power and creating a united Germany.

**Geology** An area of science that studies the solid Earth, especially minerals and rocks.

**Hinduism** An ancient religion begun in India around 3,000–2,000 BC, which has many gods, values tolerance and believes that truth comes from many places.

**Holocaust** Complete destruction or devastation on a mass scale. The Holocaust usually refers to the systematic killing of Jewish people (as well as Gypsies, the mentally ill and other minority groups) in Europe by the Nazis. Around six million Jewish people and five million other victims were killed.

**Hundred Years' War** (Approximately 1337–1453) A long-term struggle between the French and the English over many issues, especially the claim to the French throne.

**Indigenous** A person, plant or object that originates in a particular place; native.

**Industrial Revolution** (Approximately 1760–1840) The process of change from a more traditional society based on farming to a more modern one based on the use of machines, which began in Great Britain.

**Inquisition** A process of examining religious faith and testing loyalty to the Catholic church, lasting in Spain from 1478–1834, and associated with intolerance and brutal methods.

**Islam** A major religion started in the 600s by the prophet Muhammad in Arabia, which believes in giving in to the will of Allah, or God, and following the laws of the Qur'an. There are over one and a half billion Muslims in the world.

**Judaism** A religion that believes in one God called Yahweh, and follows the teachings of the Torah, made up of laws given by God to Moses and parts of the Old Testament of the Bible.

**Martyr** A person who is killed because of their beliefs, usually religious.

**Molecule** A group of atoms bonded together that is the smallest unit of a compound in chemistry.

**NASA (National Aeronautics and Space Administration)** A United States government agency started in 1958, responsible for research and exploration both within and beyond the Earth's atmosphere.

**Nazism** Also known as National Socialism, a harsh, aggressive political movement, led by the dictator Adolf Hitler, which controlled Germany from 1933-1945, and whose racist policies led to the Holocaust.

**Neoplatonism** The last school of Greek philosophy, started in the 200s, inspired by Plato's belief in unchanging, eternal ideas, and concerned with the quality of human life.

**New World** The term for the continents of North and South America, after voyages by European explorers.

**Nobel Prize** Any one of six prizes awarded every year for outstanding work in physics, chemistry, medicine, literature, economics and the promotion of peace. Funded by the Swedish inventor Alfred Nobel in the late 1800s and given by a panel of Swedish judges (or the Norwegian government for the peace prize), the prizes are generally believed to be the world's highest awards.

**Nuremburg Laws** Anti-Jewish rules set out in 1935 by Adolf Hitler and adopted in Germany, which took away German citizenship from Jewish people, stopped them marrying non-Jews, and began the repression of the Jewish people that eventually led to the Holocaust.

**Pagan** A person holding beliefs different to the main world religions, often believing in multiple gods.

**Palaeontologist** A scientist who studies fossils to understand the geological past.

**Parliament** A formal meeting to discuss public matters; the law-making part of government in the UK.

**Pesticide** A chemical substance used to destroy insects that may be harmful to plants, especially crops, or to animals.

**Physics** An area of science that studies matter and energy.

**Polio** Short for poliomyelitis, a virus that affects the central nervous system and can cause paralysis.

**Protestant** A branch of Christianity started in the Reformation in the 1500s, when Martin Luther and John Cal-vin led a movement to reject the authority of the Pope and to use the Bible as the highest authority, making the religion directly available to readers in common language.

**Qur'an (or Koran)** Sacred writings and laws believed to be given by Allah to the prophet Muhammad, forming the basis of the religion of Islam.

**Racism** Prejudice or discrimination against someone of a different skin colour or physical appearance; the belief that one's own race is superior to another.

**Radioactivity** Rays of energy or particles that are given off when atoms in an element break apart.

**Rosetta Stone** An ancient Egyptian stone with carvings in Greek, Egyptian hieroglyphs and demotic (a cursive form of hieroglyphs), which allowed scholars to decode the meaning of hieroglyphs, a form of writing in pictures, and therefore to understand much of ancient Egyptian history.

**Second World War** (1939-1945) The war fought between the Axis Powers (Germany, Italy and Japan) and the Allied Powers (France, Great Britain, United States and Russia), partly in continuation of the problems of the First World War. The Allies eventually won the war. Around 50 million people were killed.

**Segregation** The action of setting someone or something apart from others, often based on inequality, sometimes as systematic persecution set in law.

**Sharia (or shariah)** Islamic laws based on the Qur'an, outlining both religious and secular behaviour; the way in which laws are applied is debated by traditional and modern Muslims.

**Silk Road** An ancient trading route linking China and the West, carrying ideas and goods, with silk going west and wool, gold and silver going east.

**Spanish Armada** A fleet of 130 ships sent by King Phillip II of Spain in 1588, to conquer England. Many ships were blown off course by storms and sunk off the coast of Ireland, and the rest were defeated by the English naval force under Lord Charles Howard and Sir Francis Drake.

**Suffrage** The right to vote in political elections.

**Sufism** The Islamic mystic tradition in which Muslims seek divine love and knowledge through direct personal experience with Allah.

**Taliban** An ultraconservative group of Muslim extremists, started in the mid-1990s, which took over Afghanistan and imposed extremely strict rules, especially on women.

**Tuberculosis** A dangerous bacterial infection that affects the lungs, bones and central nervous system. Widespread in Europe in the 1800s, it was known as consumption, and still causes millions of deaths every year in developing nations.

**Typhus** A group of infectious diseases caused by rickettsia bacteria, often passed to humans by lice, fleas or ticks, common in crowded, dirty conditions during wars or famines, causing rashes, headaches, nausea, fever, delirium and often death.

**Underground Railroad** A network of sympathetic people that helped lead tens of thousands of black slaves out of the southern or 'Confederate' United States to safety in the North and Canada during the 1800s. Neither truly 'underground' nor an actual 'railroad', it was a system through which white abolitionists who opposed slavery, church leaders (especially Quakers), and freed black people helped slaves to escape by travelling along safe routes at night.

**United Nations** An international group of countries formed in 1945, which aims to promote peace and security in the world, establish friendly relations between member countries, support human rights, and uphold international law through cooperation and mutual respect.

**Zionism** A Jewish nationalist movement that has aimed to create and support a Jewish homeland (Eretz Yisrael in Hebrew), which was achieved in 1948 with the creation of the State of Israel, in the historical land of Palestine. It takes its name from a hill in the city of Jerusalem called Zion.

# INDEX

## A

Aboriginal people 100, 101
actor 38, 39, 44-45, 64
Africa 60, 61, 83
African American 25, 32, 33, 38, 39, 78, 94-95
  slavery 16, 17
Agnodice 62
Alexandria 72, 73
Angelou, Maya 38-39, 107
animal 29, 35, 82-83
  pet 27, 28, 31, 44
Anning, Mary 76-77, 106
Argentina 64, 65
art 26, 27, 28, 29, 31, 40, 41, 45
astronaut 79, 84-85
astronomer 70, 72
athlete 100-101
Australia 100, 101
author see writer

## B

ballet 31, 34, 35
Bernhardt, Sarah 46-47, 106
Blackwell, Elizabeth 62-63, 106
blindness 48, 49, 50, 63
blogger 87
book 28, 29, 31, 38, 39, 43, 45, 55, 57, 61, 69, 83, 87, 95, 96, 105
Boudicca 18-19, 106
Britain 10, 18, 19, 47, 77, 81, 99
Brontë, Emily 42-43, 106
Bucci, Dorotea 62

## C

Carson, Rachel 68-69, 107
Catholicism 7, 8, 23
Celtic people 18, 19
Chanel, Coco 30-31, 107
chemist 66, 67, 74, 80-81
chief 12-13
China 14, 15
civil rights 17, 38, 49, 94-95
Communist 27, 85
computer 70, 71, 80, 81
conservation 29, 60-61, 68, 83
Curie, Irène 66, 67
Curie, Marie 66-67, 106

## D, E

dance 34, 35
Davison, Emily 99
deafness 48, 49
DNA 74, 75, 80
doctor 56, 60, 62-63
Earhart, Amelia 90-91, 107
Ebadi, Shirin 54-55, 107
education 13, 15, 23, 50-51, 56-57, 61, 66, 86, 87, 94
  university 23
Egypt 20, 21, 72
Elizabeth I 6-7, 106
empire 7, 23
empress 14-15
England 7, 18, 19, 29, 43, 53
exploration 7, 23, 24-25

## F, G

farming 15, 29, 61, 68
fashion 30, 31, 45
Fossey, Dian 82-83, 107
France 9
Frank, Anne 104-105, 107
Franklin, Rosalind 74-75, 107
Freeman, Cathy 100-101, 107
Gandhi, Indira 10-11, 107
geology 76, 77
Germany 102, 103, 104
Green Belt Movement 61
Guatemala 88, 89

## H, I

Hatshepsut 20-21, 106
healthcare 46, 47, 52, 62-63, 64, 67, 75, 80, 81
Hindu faith 36-37
Hodgkin, Dorothy 80-81, 107
Holiday, Billie 32-33, 107
human rights 54, 55, 84-85
Hypatia 72-73, 106
India 10, 11, 36, 58
International Red Cross 47
Iran 54
Isabella I 22-23, 106
Italy 56, 62

## J, K

Jewish people 23, 92-93, 102
Joan of Arc 8-9, 10, 106
Johnson, Katherine 78-79, 107
Kachindamoto, Theresa 12-13, 107
Kahlo, Frida 26-27, 107
Keller, Helen 48-49, 50-51, 106
Kenya 60-61
Khan, Noor Inayat 96-97, 107

## L, M, N

Lovelace, Ada 70-71, 106
Maathai, Wangari 60-61, 107
Malawi 12, 13
marriage 7, 12, 13, 22
maths 47, 70, 71, 72, 78, 79
Mayan people 88, 89
medicine 25, 52, 80, 81
Menchú, Roberta 88-89, 107
Mirabai 36-37, 106
Montessori, Maria 56-57, 106
Mother Teresa 58-59, 107
music 32-33, 71
Muslim people 23, 54, 55
NASA 78, 79
Native American 24-25
Nightingale, Florence 46-47, 63, 106
Nobel Prizes 66, 67, 75, 81
  Peace 55, 57, 59, 61, 87, 89
nurse 17, 29, 46-47, 52, 53, 99

## O, P, Q

O'Keeffe, Georgia 40-41, 107
painter 26-27, 28, 40-41
Pakistan 86, 87
Pankhurst, Emmeline 98-99, 106
Parks, Rosa 94-95, 107
Pavlova, Anna 34-35, 107
Perón, Eva 64-65, 107
pharaoh 20-21
philosopher 72
pilot 90-91
poet 36, 39, 43, 92
politics 10-11, 15, 64
Potter, Beatrix 28-29, 106
poverty 12, 13, 32, 33, 50, 58, 76
Presidential Medal of Freedom 79, 95
prime minister 11
prison 7, 9, 11, 23, 55
queen 7, 18, 22-23

## R, S

Ride, Sally 85
Russia 34, 84
Sacajawea 24–25, 106
saint 9, 37
Scholl, Sophie 102–103, 107
scientist 61, 66–69, 74–77, 80–81
Seacole, Mary 52–53, 106
singer 30, 32–33, 36, 92
slavery 16, 17, 23, 52, 62
Somerville, Mary 70
space 11, 79, 84–85
Spain 22, 23
sport 26, 100–101

spy 15, 17, 93, 97
suffragette 98–99
Sullivan, Annie 48, 49, 50–51, 106
Szenes, Hannah 92–93, 107

## T, U, V

Tereshkova, Valentina 84–85, 107
Tubman, Harriet 16–17, 106
Underground Railroad 16
UNESCO ambassador 87
USA 16, 17, 24, 25, 32, 33, 40, 41, 63, 84, 94–95
voting 25, 65, 98–99

## W, Y

war 8–9, 11, 22–23, 44
   American Civil War 17
   Crimean War 46, 53
   First World War 45, 67, 99
   Second World War 93, 96–97, 104–105
White Rose 102, 103
writer 28, 29, 39, 42–43, 49, 53, 61, 68–69, 83, 87, 89, 96, 105
Wu Zeitan 14–15, 106
Yousafzai, Malala 86–87, 107

## Acknowledgements

(Key: a-above; b-below/bottom; c-centre; f-far; l-left; r-right; t-top)

6 GL Archive/Alamy Stock Photo (tl); Artokoloro Quint Lox Limited/Alamy Stock Photo (tr). 7 Skyscan Photolibrary/Alamy Stock Photo (c); Chronicle/Alamy Stock Photo (br). 9 Holmes Garden Photos/Alamy Stock Photo (tr). 10 World History Archive/Alamy Stock Photo (tr). 11 Carl Mydans/The LIFE Picture Collection/Getty Images (bl). 12 © UN Women (tl). 13 robertharding/Alamy Stock Photo (cr). 14 © Aptyp_koK/Shutterstock.com (ml). 15 © sofiaworld/Shutterstock.com (tl); ART Collection/Alamy Stock Photo (br). 16 Pictorial Press Ltd/Alamy Stock Photo (tr). 17 Artepics/Alamy Stock Photo (tr). 19 © Philip Bird LRPS CPAGB/Shutterstock.com (bl). 20 © Maciek67/Shuterstock.com (br). 22 Granger Historical Picture Archive/Alamy Stock Photo (tr). 23 Granger Historical Picture Archive/Alamy Stock Photo (tl). 25 Everett Historical/Shutterstock.com (tl); Everett Historical/Shutterstock.com (tr); Witold Skrypczak/Alamy Stock Photo (cr). 27 CSU Archives/Everett Collection Historical/Alamy Stock Photo (tl); Granger Historical Picture Archive/Alamy Stock Photo (r). 28 WorldPhotos/Alamy Stock Photo (tr). 29 Annie Eagle/Alamy Stock Photo (br; fr). 31 flavia raddavero/Alamy Stock Photo (tl); Granger Historical Picture Archive/Alamy Stock Photo (tr). 32 Pictorial Press Ltd/Alamy Stock Photo (tl). 33 Everett Collection Inc/Alamy Stock Photo (cr). 34 Paul Fearn/Alamy Stock Photo (tl); Heritage Image Partnership Ltd/Alamy Stock Photo (br). 35 INTERFOTO/Alamy Stock Photo (bl). 36 IndiaPicture/Alamy Stock Photo (tr); ephotocorp/Alamy Stock Photo (bl). 37 Dinodia Photos/Alamy Stock Photo (br). 38 Everett Collection Historical/Alamy Stock Photo (tl); CBW/Alamy Stock Photo (cl). 39 Jeff Morgan 11/Alamy Stock Photo (bl). 40 Granger Historical Picture Archive/Alamy Stock Photo (tl); Heritage Image Partnership Ltd/Alamy Stock Photo (bl). 41 Everett Collection Inc/Alamy Stock Photo (tl). 42 Art Collection 4/Alamy Stock Photo (tr). 43 Wild Life Ranger/Alamy Stock Photo (br); Lebrecht Music and Arts Photo Library/Alamy Stock Photo (fbr). 44 Everett Historical/Shutterstock.com (tr). 45 Chronicle/Alamy Stock Photo (tl). 46 IanDagnall Computing/Alamy Stock Photo (tl); Picture/Alamy Stock Photo (bl). 47 Hulton Archive/Stringer/Getty Images (cr); Prisma by Dukas Presseagentur GmbH/Alamy Stock Photo (br). 48 Everett Collection Historical/Alamy Stock Photo (tr); Granger Historical Picture Archive/Alamy Stock Photo (cr). 49 INTERFOTO/Alamy Stock Photo (tr). 50 Granger Historical Picture Archive/Alamy Stock Photo (tr). 51 Everett Collection Historical/Alamy Stock Photo (br). 53 Private Collection/Bridgeman Images (cl); GL Archive/Alamy Stock Photo (br). 54 Sipa Press/REX/Shutterstock (tr). 55 Marco Destefanis/Alamy Stock Photo (tr). 56 Chronicle/Alamy Stock Photo (tl); Bettmann/Getty Images (cr). 57 Nenov Brothers Images (tl); Kurt Hutton/Stringer/Picture Post/Getty Images (b). 58 Vittoriano Rastelli/Corbis via Getty Images (tr). 59 Keystone Pictures USA/Alamy Stock Photo (tr); Joerg Boethling/Alamy Stock Photo (cr). 61 SIMON MAINA/AFP/Getty Images (tl); Wendy Stone/Corbis via Getty Images (br). 62 Pictorial Press Ltd/Alamy Stock Photo (tl). 63 Granger Historical Picture Archive/Alamy Stock Photo (tl); Everett Collection Historical/Alamy Stock Photo (cr). 64 Pictorial Press Ltd/Alamy Stock Photo (tr); Everett Collection Inc/Alamy Stock Photo (bl). 65 Everett Collection Inc/Alamy Stock Photo (br). 66 Everett Historical/Shutterstock.com (tl). 67 Paul Fearn/Alamy Stock Photo (c); Wellcome Collection (br). 68 JHU Sheridan Libraries/Gado/Getty Images (tr); Alfred Eisenstaedt/The LIFE Picture Collection/Getty Images (cl); sjbooks/Alamy Stock Photo (bl). 69 Everett Collection Inc/Alamy Stock Photo (tl). 70 ART Collection/Alamy Stock Photo (tl); GL Archive/Alamy Stock Photo (br). 73 National Geographic Creative/Alamy Stock Photo (tl); Science History Images/Alamy Stock Photo (bl). 74 Science History Images/Alamy Stock Photo (bl). 75 World History Archive/Alamy Stock Photo (br). 76 Private Collection/© Look and Learn/Bridgeman Images (tl); 76–77 The Natural History Museum/Alamy Stock Photo (b). 77 The Natural History Museum/Alamy Stock Photo (bl). 78 Science History Images/Alamy Stock Photo (tl). 79 NASA/Donaldson Collection/Getty Images (bl). 80 Keystone Pictures USA/Alamy Stock Photo (tl); Jennie Mills/Science Museum/SSPL/Getty Images (cr). 81 Mondadori Portfolio via Getty Images (br). 82 United News/Popperfoto/Getty Images (tr). 83 Liam White/Alamy Stock Photo (tl). 84 SPUTNIK/Alamy Stock Photo (tl); severjn/Shutterstock.com (tr). 85 SPUTNIK/Alamy Stock Photo (cr); SPUTNIK/Alamy Stock Photo (br). 86 Oli Scarff/AFP/Getty Images (l). 87 Splash News/Alamy Stock Photo (r). 88 incamerastock/Alamy Stock Photo (tr). 90 B Christopher/Alamy Stock Photo (tl); © KEYSTONE Pictures/ZUMAPRESS.com (br). 91 John Frost Newspapers/Alamy Stock Photo (b). 92 Heritage Image Partnership Ltd/Alamy Stock Photo (bl). 93 War Archive/Alamy Stock Photo (cr). 94 Everett Collection Historical/Alamy Stock Photo (cl). 95 Granger Historical Picture Archive/Alamy Stock Photo (bl). 96 © IWM (HU 74868) (tr); Mophart Creation/Shutterstock.com (bl); Basement Stock/Alamy Stock Photo (bc). 97 dominic dibbs/Alamy Stock Photo (bl). 98 Archive Pics/Alamy Stock Photo (cl); Archive Pics/Alamy Stock Photo (tr). 99 World History Archive/Alamy Stock Photo (tr). 100 Theodore Liasi/Alamy Stock Photo (tr). 101 Allstar Picture Library/Alamy Stock Photo (cr). 102 INTERFOTO/Alamy Stock Photo (tr); Alan Copson City Pictures/Alamy Stock Photo (bl). 103 INTERFOTO/Alamy Stock Photo (bl). 104 Heritage Image Partnership Ltd/Alamy Stock Photo (tl); Heritage Image Partnership Ltd/Alamy Stock Photo (cl); Everett Collection Inc/Alamy Stock Photo (cr). 105 DPA picture alliance archive/Alamy Stock Photo (cr); Andreas Arnold/DPA picture alliance/Alamy Stock Photo (br).

# BELIEVE & LEAD

What makes a great leader? Is it bravery or belief? Cleverness or conviction? Power or personality? The women in this chapter come from many countries, historical periods and backgrounds, but they all shared one dream: the desire to create a better world. While fighting to prove that women were just as capable of leading as men, they broke boundaries with their intelligence, dedication and belief that they could make a difference. Their leadership shook the world.

# IMAGINE & CREATE

What makes a great artist? Is it talent or tenacity? Brilliance or boldness? Wit or wisdom? The women in this chapter shared many and sometimes all of these gifts. Their inventiveness and willingness to try new things helped them to create amazing art, whether with pictures, words, movement or song. Inspiring those around them, these women and their amazing creations continue to move, motivate and connect with us today. Their art shook the world.

# HELP & HEAL

What makes a great guide, teacher or healer? Is it commitment or compassion? Service or sacrifice? Generosity or gentleness? The answer is, of course, all of these and more. The women in this chapter spent their lives improving the lives of others; tending to the ill, the injured, the poor and those in need. Many made huge sacrifices in order to help those less fortunate than themselves, and the work they started continues to change lives to this day. Their compassion shook the world.

# THINK & SOLVE

What makes a great problem-solver? Is it intelligence or ingenuity? Originality or optimism? Daring or dedication? The women in this chapter possess all of these traits, as their curiosity and inventiveness drove them to ask questions and seek answers. Despite being told that the world of science and maths was for men and men only, these amazing women proved that the pursuit of truth and knowledge belongs to us all, equally, no matter who we are or where we come from. Their courageous and clever problem-solving shook the world.

# HOPE & OVERCOME

What makes a great hero, fighter or dreamer? Is it courage or confidence? Fearlessness or faith? Strength or spirit? The women in this chapter shared all of these qualities and more. They were fighters even when they could not win. They were survivors even when they did not live. They were believers that things could and would change, even if they wouldn't get to see it. And the greatest thing they shared — indeed with all of the women in this book — was hope.

### THEY SHOOK THE WORLD